First World War
and Army of Occupation
War Diary
France, Belgium and Germany

50 DIVISION
149 Infantry Brigade
Royal Fusiliers (City of London Regiment)
3rd Battalion
1 July 1918 - 31 May 1919

WO95/2831/2

The Naval & Military Press Ltd
www.nmarchive.com
Published in association with The National Archives

Published by

The Naval & Military Press Ltd

Unit 10 Ridgewood Industrial Park,

Uckfield, East Sussex,

TN22 5QE England

Tel: +44 (0) 1825 749494

www.naval-military-press.com

www.nmarchive.com

This diary has been reprinted in facsimile from the original. Any imperfections are inevitably reproduced and the quality may fall short of modern type and cartographic standards.

© **Crown Copyright**
Images reproduced by permission of The National Archives, London, England, 2015.

Contents

Document type	Place/Title	Date From	Date To
Heading	WO95/2831 3rd Battalion Royal Fusiliers July 1918-May 1919		
Heading	50th Division 149th Infy Bde 3rd Bn Royal Fusiliers July 1918-May 1919 From Salonika 85 Bde 28 Div		
War Diary	Braio Rest Camp.	01/07/1918	01/07/1918
War Diary	Itea. Rest Camp	01/07/1918	02/07/1918
War Diary	French Transport Timgad.	03/07/1918	03/07/1918
War Diary	Taranto. Rest Camp.	04/07/1918	04/07/1918
War Diary	Troop Train TF.21.	05/07/1918	09/07/1918
War Diary	Martin. Eglise Camp	10/07/1918	15/07/1918
War Diary	Martin Eglise Camp No 4.	16/07/1918	31/07/1918
Miscellaneous	3rd. Battalion Royal Fusiliers.	12/07/1918	12/07/1918
Miscellaneous		12/07/1918	12/07/1918
Miscellaneous	3rd. Battalion Royal Fusiliers. Roll of Officers shewing short Record of Service.	12/07/1918	12/07/1918
Miscellaneous	3rd. Battalion Royal Fusiliers.	12/07/1918	12/07/1918
Heading	War Diary 3rd Bn Royal Fusiliers for Month of August 1918 Vol 3		
War Diary	Martin Eglise Camp. No 4.	01/08/1918	31/08/1918
Heading	War Diary 3rd Bn Royal Fusiliers October 1918. 3 Appendices. Vol 5		
War Diary	Battln Hqrs Nurlu Sheet 62C 1/40,000 Co Ord. D4B.6.6.	01/10/1918	01/10/1918
War Diary	Bn Hqrs. Montbreain Ea1A 1/20,000 F5.B.5.5.	02/10/1918	03/10/1918
War Diary	Montbrehain Ed1A 1/20,000	04/10/1918	06/10/1918
War Diary	Bn HQ Trenches Vauxhall Inary.	07/10/1918	07/10/1918
War Diary	Bn. HQ. Guisancourt Farm T27C4.0)	08/10/1918	10/10/1918
War Diary	Bn. HQ. Maurois. P.22B Ref. France Sheet 57B	11/10/1918	11/10/1918
War Diary	Bn. HQ Maurois.	12/10/1918	12/10/1918
War Diary	Bn HQ Honnechy	13/10/1918	14/10/1918
War Diary	Bn HQ. Honnechy.	15/10/1918	16/10/1918
War Diary	Map Ref. Sheet 57B 1/40,000	17/10/1918	18/10/1918
War Diary	Bn. HQ Maretz France Sheet 57B. U.6.	19/10/1918	19/10/1918
War Diary	Bn HQ Maretz	20/10/1918	29/10/1918
War Diary	B.N. HQ Reumont	29/10/1918	29/10/1918
War Diary	Bn HQ L19b50 Refe Map 57b	30/10/1918	30/10/1918
War Diary	Bn HQ Fontaine Au Bois	31/10/1918	31/10/1918
Operation(al) Order(s)	3rd Battalion Royal Fusiliers Order No.2.	16/10/1918	16/10/1918
Operation(al) Order(s)	3rd Battalion Royal Fusiliers Addenda to Order No.2.	16/10/1918	16/10/1918
Heading	War Diary 3rd Battalion Royal Fusiliers. November-1918 Appendices 13. Maps 2. Vol 6		
War Diary		31/10/1918	06/11/1918
War Diary	Petit Landrecies C15D.5.8.	06/11/1918	06/11/1918
War Diary	C11D.9.3.	06/11/1918	06/11/1918
War Diary	Rombise Farm.	06/11/1918	09/11/1918
War Diary	Bn H.Q. Mont Dourlers	10/11/1918	30/11/1918
Miscellaneous	3rd. Royal Fusiliers. Preliminary Instruction. No. 1. Appendix No. I.	02/11/1918	02/11/1918
Miscellaneous	3rd. Battalion Royal Fusiliers. Order of Battle-November 1st. 1918.	01/11/1918	01/11/1918

Type	Description	From	To
Miscellaneous	3rd Royal Fusiliers. Preliminary Instruction-No. 2. Appendix. 4.		
Operation(al) Order(s)	3rd. Royal Fusiliers. Operation Order No. 4. Appendix 6.	03/11/1918	03/11/1918
Miscellaneous	O.C. No. 2. Coy. Somi. Appendix No. 7.	04/11/1918	04/11/1918
Miscellaneous	3rd. Battalion Royal Fusiliers. Battalion Orders. Appendix. 8.	04/11/1918	04/11/1918
Map	France.		
Map	France. Enemy Rear Organisation.		
Operation(al) Order(s)	3rd. Royal Fusiliers. Order-No. 5. Appendix 1.	05/11/1918	05/11/1918
Operation(al) Order(s)	Appendix. 1. 3rd. Royal Fusiliers, Order No. 6.	06/11/1918	06/11/1918
Miscellaneous	Appendix. 1. Message of congratulation received from the Army Commander and Divisional Commander, November 7th, 1918.	07/11/1918	07/11/1918
Miscellaneous	Orders issued to O.C. No. 2. Company, Nov. 6th, 1918. Appendix. 2.	06/11/1918	06/11/1918
Miscellaneous	Appendix 3. Message to 149th. Infy. Brigade from 3rd Royal Fusiliers.		
Miscellaneous	Appendix. 1. To Buze R.F. 63.		
Miscellaneous	Appendix. 2. To O.C. No. 2. Company.		
Miscellaneous	Appendix. 3. Message from 3rd Royal Fusiliers to 149 Inf. Brigade.		
Heading	War Diary. 3rd Battalion Royal Fusiliers. December-1918. Appendices-Nil. Vol 7		
War Diary	Dourlers.	01/12/1918	04/12/1918
War Diary	Battn. Hqrs. Dompierre. Map. 57A J7A.13	05/12/1918	05/12/1918
War Diary	Dompierre.	05/12/1918	18/12/1918
War Diary	Le Quesnoy	18/12/1918	31/12/1918
Heading	War Diary 3rd Royal Fusiliers. Appendices, Nil January 1919 Vol 8		
War Diary	Le Quesnoy	01/01/1919	31/01/1919
Heading	War Diary 3rd Royal Fusiliers. February-1919 Appendices-Nil. Vol 9		
War Diary	Le Quesnoy	01/02/1919	28/02/1919
Heading	War Diary. 3rd Bn. Royal Fusiliers. March 1919. Vol 10		
War Diary	Le-Quesnoy	01/03/1919	31/03/1919
Heading	3rd. Battalion Royal Fusiliers. War Diary. April, 1919. Vol 11		
War Diary	Le-Quesnoy.	01/04/1919	30/04/1919
Heading	War Diary. 3rd Battalion Royal Fusiliers. May 1919. Vol 12		
War Diary	Le Quesnoy	01/05/1919	31/05/1919
Map	France		
Miscellaneous	France. Sheet 57A Edition 1.		

(2) WO95/2831

3rd Battalion Royal Fusiliers

July 1918 – May 1919

50TH DIVISION
149TH INFY BDE

3RD BN ROYAL FUSILIERS
JLY 1918 - MAY 1919

From Salonika
85 Bde 28 Div

3RD BATTALION ROYAL FUSILIERS – JULY – VOLUME II.

WAR DIARY
or
INTELLIGENCE SUMMARY.

(Erase heading not required.)   3rd Battalion Royal Fusiliers

Army Form C. 2118.

Instructions regarding War Diaries and Intelligence Summaries are contained in F. S. Regs., Part II. and the Staff Manual respectively. Title pages will be prepared in manuscript.

Place	Date	Hour	Summary of Events and Information	Remarks and references to Appendices
BRALO REST CAMP	July 1st 1918		Tps. 3rd Companies +Hqrs detrained at BRALO & marched to Rest Camp. Nos. 1,4,2 Companies and Transport arrived Bestonias on 30th inst. The Battalion proceeded to ITEA by motor lorry at 1400 hours – 40 lorries +5 Baggage lorries being provided – these latter proceeded at 1230 with Instructions – advance party. 17 officers) attached to Battalion 4 Y.M.C.A. officials) 26. O.R's Battalion arrived ITEA at 1800 hrs & proceeded to Rest Camp. 3. O.R's were admitted to Hospital at BRALO. Strength of Battn (excluding attached) 72 officers 796 O.R.S.	
ITEA. REST CAMP.	2nd		at ITEA rest Camp	
"	3rd		Embarked on French Transport "TIMGAD" at 0530. Left TARANTO Gulf at 0715. Baggage Completed without incident	
FRENCH TRANSPORT TIMGAD.	4		arrived TARANTO at 0800 entrained inner harbour & disembarked at 1130. and proceeded to TARANTO REST CAMP. entrained on T.F.21 for SERQUEUX (FRANCE) at 1830 hrs. 8 Officers 1277. O.R 2/20 Sussex Regt. +26 others attached	

WAR DIARY
or
~~INTELLIGENCE SUMMARY~~
(Erase heading not required.)

3Rd Battalion Royal Fusiliers

Army Form C. 2118.

Instructions regarding War Diaries and Intelligence Summaries are contained in F.S. Regs, Part II. and the Staff Manual respectively. Title pages will be prepared in manuscript.

Place	Date	Hour	Summary of Events and Information	Remarks and references to Appendices
TROOP TRAIN T.F. 21.	July 5: 1918.		Travelled via East Coast Route, passing BARI, FOGGIA, CASTLEMARIA, ANCONA.	
	6.		(to FAENZA. 2 hours halt.) Thence via BOLOGNA to SAMPIERDIERNA. Capt A.S. ARGENT evacuated sick MALARIA. 17 7th inst at 1800 hrs.	
	7.		Along Riviera. SAVONA to CANNES.	
	8.		Battalion Bathed in Sea at CANNES on 9th at 0600. MARSEILLES. 1400 hrs. MIRAMAS.	
	9.		LYONS, ST GERMAINS, MONT DOR. PARAY LE MONAIL. Thence to MAISHERBES to JUVISY and BEAUVAIS, Et.	
	10.		arrived SERQUEUX at 1830. O.R's O. intended but to proceed to ARQUES LA BATAILLE – 2/20 London Regt detrained with arrived ARQUES LA BATAILLE at 2015. and dismounted but to proceed. Marches to MARTIN EGLISE Camp	
MARTIN EGLISE CAMP.			No 13 arriving in camp at 2215. Strength Marching into camp, 18 officers + 740 O.R's following officers admitted hospital not with. LIEUT R.A.L. DAVIES D.C. CORLETT A.S. BALDING	
	11.		In camp, arranging fatigues + sitting down. Holding Lecture Experiments. 2 hours of 2½ days each LIEUT J.A. TURNER down leave to U.K.	
	12.		Practice Ceremonial Parade for 14. duties with for Parade on 14 inst	
	13.		4 men sent daily on 14 days leave to UK commencing this day.	
	14.		French National Site day – 3/Royal Fusiliers, 1/Royal. 2/17Lancers. 2/8 Dub Fusiliers each Battn 400 Strong marched through DIEPPE to the PLACE. formed up in line & reviewed by MAJOR GENERAL. H.C. JACKSON. D.S.O. Commanding 50? Division. Battalion marched past in Column of Companies + in Quarter Column – Brig General P.M. ROBINSON A.G.O. c/Hq Bde. Commanding the Parade – on return to camp. Battalion marches past. G.H.Q. GENERAL SIR. H. RAWLINSON. K.C.B. G.C.S. + G.T. along – and	
	15.		Camp Moved to The 4 Camp. MARTIN. EGLISE. – are work of erecting camp. Continue	

Commenced.

Army Form C. 2118.

WAR DIARY
or
INTELLIGENCE SUMMARY.
(Erase heading not required.)

3rd Battalion Royal Fusiliers

Place	Date	Hour	Summary of Events and Information	Remarks and references to Appendices
MARTIN TENTS CAMP No 4.	July 16. 1918		Platoon Training under company & Platoon commanders. Work of exciting. Route March by companies. Marching over. Lewis gun anti-aircraft position commences.	cook Parades. Ablution Sheds Latrines - Refuse pits Salvage pits Incinerators
	17		continued	continued under Regt. Pioneers
	18		continued	LIEUT R.A.L. DAVIES) Returned LIEUT D.C. CORLETT) from Hospital
	19		Work of digging 2 feet deep & building up first to give protection against hostile aircraft commenced. Training together work continued.	
	20		Work of digging in tents continued - completed.	
	21st		Lewis gun anti aircraft positions completed	Capt R.M. LARGE re-joined from Leave to U.K.
	22nd		Platoon training according to programme under Company & Platoon Commanders Capt. REV F. Smith attached to the Battalion from this date	
	23rd		work continued on	Col. Parsons completed
	24 d		"	Salvage pit & ablution sheds
	25 d		"	"
	26 d		"	"
	27 d			LIEUT D.C. CORLETT proceeds on Leave (14 days) to U.K.

Army Form C. 2118.

WAR DIARY
or
INTELLIGENCE SUMMARY.
(Erase heading not required.)

3rd Battalion Royal Fusiliers

Place	Date	Hour	Summary of Events and Information	Remarks and references to Appendices
MARTIN EGLISE Camp No 4	July 28th 1918		Parade Church service at 1100 hours for the Battalion.	
	29th		Platoon + Company training - continuation of constructional work on Camp.	
	30th		30 yds Range Completed. Tps. 1+4 Companies fired on sand Training continued with remaining companies. Tps 2+3 firing on Ranges.	
	31st		½ Battalion Route March for 3 hours.	

Strength. 19 officers. 622 O.R's excluding attached
attached 2 officers 25 O.R's

evacuated to Hospital during month of July:
Malaria. 20. O.R.S.
other causes. 66. O.R.S.

3 officers evacuated N.Y.D. Pyrexia - Malaria
2 since re-joined.

[signature]
Lt. Col
Commanding 3rd Battn Royal Fusiliers

[signature] Humphreys Capt
Adjutant 3rd Battn Royal Fusiliers

3rd. Battalion Royal Fusiliers.

Where majority of men were enlisted:- London District. ~~Staffordshire.~~

Date of Battalion proceeding overseas:- 18.1.1915.

Short history of Battalion:- Attached.

Health of Battalion:- *Has suffered much from Malaria.*

Nomina-l Roll of Officers shewing short
Record of Service:- Attached.

Summary of Men shewing period
on Service without Leave:- Attached.

Lt. Colonel.
Commanding 3rd. Battalion Royal Fusiliers.

12.7.1918.

Short History of War Service of 3rd Battalion Royal Fusiliers.
(ex 85th Brigade, 28th Division)

The Battalion embarked for France on January 18th, 1915.
Took part in 2nd battle of YPRES- April and May, 1915, and battle of LOOS- Sept, 1915. (Hohenzollern Redoubt)
In both these actions the Battalion suffered very heavily.

Embarked for Egypt in October 1915.

Embarked for Salonika in November 1915.

Battalion employed from December 1915 till April 1916 in construction of portion of Salonika Defences.

June 1916 marched to Struma Valley where Battalion suffered very heavily from Malaria. Moved back to Hills in July 1916.

Occupied trenches near Butkovo in October 1916.

Occupied trenches in front of BARAKLI DZUMA February 1917- June 1917 when Struma Valley was evacuated for reasons of health.

During May 1917 the Battalion took part in operations which resulted in capture of Ferdie Trench, a portion of enemy outpost line.
75 prisoners and a Machine Gun were taken during the period covered by these operations. Our total casualties being 2 Officers and 80 other ranks.

July 1917. Held sector of British Line along KRUSA BALKAN, East of Lake DOIRAN till September 1917 when Brigade marched back to Struma.

October 1917. Crossed Struma River and took up Outpost Line in the old British Front Line of previous winter.. This line was held in turn by one Battalion in front line, with 3 Battalions in reserve..
The Outpost Line consisted of a series of Redoubts covering a front of about 4,000 yards; the line of Resistance being on right bank of River Struma.
During the period the Battalion was out of the Outpost Line, 3 days work on defences and three days training- consisting mainly of open warfare-was carried out weekly.
Many offensive patrols were carried out across SALONIKA-CONSTANTINOPLE Railway which was approximately 6,000 yards in advance of the Outpost Line. During these operations some prisoners were captured. All these patrols were carried out by night.

March 1918. Marched over to KRUSA BALKAN Line, East of Lake DOIRAN and held a portion of this until receipt of orders to proceed to France.

Lt. Colonel.

12.7.1918.   Commanding 3rd. Battalion Royal Fusiliers.

3rd. Battalion Royal Fusiliers.

Roll of Officers shewing short Record of Service.

Rank & Name.	Date of Commission.	Service abroad Yrs.	Mths.	Period in Hospital.	Awards	Date last in U.K
Lt. Col. E.H.Nicholson	4.8.00	2	9	Nil	D.S.O.	15.7.17.
2nd in Command to 3rd. R. Fus. November 1915- May 1916. Comdg. 3rd. R. Fus:- 2nd in Command to 2nd E. Surrey.Regt. July 16-Dec.16 29.4.18. Commanding 2nd E. Surrey Regt. December 16- April 18.						
Major W. A. Trasenster	12.2.12.	2	7	3 months.	M.C.	20.3.18
A/2nd in Command 17.1.17-4.6.17. 2nd in Command 4.6.17.to date.						
Captain A. Mc. N. Gordon	24.3.15.	2	9	2 weeks	Nil.	8.5.18.
Captain R.D.T.Woolfe	13.5.15. (From Ranks)	2	6	Nil	M.in D.	10.1.16.
Captain R.T. C.C-Chadwick.	19.6.15.	2	1	10 days	Nil	26.11.16
Lieut. J. Hart.	3.5.15.	2	-	1 month	Nil	30.4.18.
Lt. C.H.Bailhache	19.5.15.	2	9	Nil	Nil	8.10.15
Lieut. W.E. Forster	2.4.16. (From ranks)	3	7	3 weeks	Nil	4.10.17.
2/Lieut. C.E.P. Cross	15.11.16. (From Ranks)	3	6	Nil	Nil	30.4.18.
2/Lieut. G.P. Nunan	15.11.16. (From ranks)	3	6	6 weeks	Nil	12.3.18.
2/Lieut. I.T. Morris	30.5.17.	-	11	6 weeks	Nil	15.8.17.
2/Lieut H. Marsh	1.8.17. (From ranks)	-	10	3 weeks	Nil	20.11.17.
2/Lieut. G.C.White.	29.1.18. (From ranks)	2	2	Nil	Croix de Guerre	29.3.18.
2/Lieut. H.L.Bronkhorst	31.1.18.	1	4	5 months	Nil	1.5.18.
2/Lieut. H.J. Savours	28.3.17.	-	5	1 month	Nil	29.5.18.
Hon. Capt.& Qr.Mr. W. Moss	24.2.12. ✓	3	1	3 months	D.C.M.	1.2.17.
Capt. & Adjt. W.T.Humphreys	13.12.15. ✓	2	9	2 weeks	Nil	1.5.18
Appointed Adjutant 12.7.1917.						
Capt. J.M. McLaggan R.A.M.C.	22.8.14. ✓	2.	10.	Nil	M.C.	13.9.17.

EHNicholson
Lt. Colonel.
Commanding 3rd. Battalion Royal Fusiliers.

12.7.1918.

3rd. Battalion Royal Fusiliers.

Return shewing Number of Other Ranks who have been on Service without Leave, for a period of One Month, upwards.

No. of Months.	No. of O.R.s	No. of Months.	No. of O.R.s
1	738	21	383
2	735	22	306
3	724	23	269
4	721	✗ 24	249
5	719	25	244
6	708	26	241
7	662	27	240
8	614	28	240
9	603	29	240
10	599	30	239
11	598	31	239
✗ 12	596	32	229
13	581	33	184
14	573	34	140
15	561	35	131
16	551	✗ 36	98
17	541	✗ 37-40	86
✗ 18	523		
19	501		
20	441		

12.7.1918.

Lt. Colonel.
Commanding 3rd. Battalion Royal Fusiliers.

SECRET

W III 3

War Diary
3rd Bn Royal Fusiliers
for Month of August 1918

WIII/8

A.H.C.
(5 sheets)

Army Form C. 2118.

WAR DIARY
or
INTELLIGENCE SUMMARY.
(Erase heading not required.)

3rd Battalion Royal Fusiliers.

Instructions regarding War Diaries and Intelligence Summaries are contained in F. S. Regs., Part II. and the Staff Manual respectively. Title pages will be prepared in manuscript.

Place	Date	Hour	Summary of Events and Information	Remarks and references to Appendices
MARTIN EGLISE Camp No 4.	August 1st 1918.		Battn. on Company training — camp improvements.	REF MAP. DIEPPE sheet 1/100,000
		2 nd.	Battn. on Duty — working parties under Brigade orders.	
		3 Rd.	2/Lt A F GOWERS D.C.M. rejoined from leave in U.K. Company training.	
		4 th	LIEUT A S BALDING rejoined from hospital. Church Service =; "Parade for 4th August".	
		5 th.	Battn. on Duty:— working parties under Brigade orders. Demonstration of attack formations to officers + W.C.O's Company training	
		6 th.		
		7 th.	Capt. & Qrmr W. MOSS. admitted to Hospital, sick.	
		8 th.	Battn. on Duty:— working parties under Brigade orders	
		9 th.	Company training	
		10 th.	Divisional tactical exercises with troops. attack through forest D'ARQUES	
		11 th.	Battn. on. Duty. LIEUT B.W TANNER. rejoined from leave U.K. Capt. D.T. WOOLFE. } proceeded special leave " B.J. O'CONNOR. rejoined. LIEUT. C H BAILHACHE. } 3 Weeks to U.K. on the 1/LT D H SWEETMAN hospital LIEUT. R.A.L. DAVIES. 10th inst.	
		12 "	Brigade tactical scheme — Regimental staff + company commanders. LIEUT. D.S. CORLETT. rejoined from leave in U.K.	

Army Form C. 2118.

WAR DIARY
or
INTELLIGENCE SUMMARY.
(Erase heading not required.)

3rd. Battn. Royal Fusiliers

Place	Date	Hour	Summary of Events and Information	Remarks and references to Appendices
MARTIN EGLISE CAMP. N°4	August 13th 1918		Capt. R.T.C. CHADWICK. proceeded on leave to U.K. Company training	
	14th		LIEUT. COL. E.H NICHOLSON. D.S.O. proceeded on leave to U.K. MAJOR W.A. TRASEMSTER. M.O. took over command of Battalion during his absence. R.S.M. HEALY. D.C.M. proceeded on leave to U.K. C.S.M. G COLBORN. took over duties of acting R.S.M during his absence. Battn. on Duty. Working parties details under Brigade orders.	
	15th		Capt. J.M McLAGGAN M.O. (R.A.M.C) att. proceeded on leave to U.K. Capt. D.C. SCOTT (R.A.M.C) att. SCOTTISH HORSE. took over duties as M.O. during his absence. Brigade tactical scheme – "outpost" area, ST AUBIN LE CAUF, BOIS D'ARCHELLES.	REF MAP DIEPPE. 1/100.000
	16th		LIEUT. B.J. O'CONNER. proceeded on leave to U.K. 2/LT D H SWEETMAN admitted hospital	
	17th		LIEUT. A.S. BALDING. proceeded on leave to U.K. Battn. on Duty. working parties detailed under Brigade orders	
	18th		50th DIVISIONAL HORSE SHOW. held on DIEPPE Race course. "sine die" all principal Civilians of DIEPPE + French Authorities attended. 3rd Royal Fusiliers. team of 6 riders won Driving Competition. for 149 Brigade. 2/LT I T MORRIS. proceeded on leave to U.K. LIEUT. E.C NEPEAN rejoined Battalion on re-posting after leave in U.K.	

Army Form C. 2118.

WAR DIARY
or
INTELLIGENCE SUMMARY

(Erase heading not required.)

3rd Battalion Royal Fusiliers

Instructions regarding War Diaries and Intelligence Summaries are contained in F.S. Regs., Part II. and the Staff Manual respectively. Title pages will be prepared in manuscript.

Place	Date	Hour	Summary of Events and Information	Remarks and references to Appendices
MARTIN EGLISE CAMP No 4.	August 19th		The following officers joined the Battn from U.K on the 18th inst: 2/Lt A.C.D PALMER. 2/Lt A.G O'NEILL. 2/Lt W P CASTON. 2/Lt A.D CALDER. = E.W. BONE. = J.W. ROBERTS. = J.J. LAWS. = A.F. LEATHERBY. = T. OGDEN. = J.M. SMITH. = B.R.C. ROGERS. all from 6th Reserve Battalion	REF. MAP DIEPPE D1/100000
	20th		LIEUT. F. PARKER. rejoined Battalion from hospital SALONIKA (wounded). Battn on Duty working parties detailed near Brigade area.	
	21st		LIEUT. W.E. FORSTER proceeded on leave to U.K.	
	21st		LIEUT. F. PARKER proceeded on leave to U.K.	
	22nd/		LIEUT. H. MARSH proceeded on leave to U.K.	
	23rd.		Battn on Duty, working parties detailed under Brigade area.	
	24th.		Company training.	
	25th.		CAPT. & adjutant W.T.HUMPHREYS. proceeded to Brigade Headquarters for temporary attachment. LIEUT. S.A TURNER took over duties of A/ADJUTANT.	
	26th		Battn on duty. Working parties detailed under Brigade Orders.	
	27th		2/LIEUT. D.H. SWEETMAN rejoined from Hospital.	
	28th		Battn did Tactical march to L.E & PUITS. Practised field firing &c.	
	29th		Battn on duty – Working parties under Brigade orders &c.	

Army Form C. 2118.

WAR DIARY
or
INTELLIGENCE SUMMARY

3rd Battalion Royal Fusiliers

Place	Date	Hour	Summary of Events and Information	Remarks and references to Appendices
MARTIN EGLISE CAMP No 4	Aug 30th 1918		Company training	
	31st		Company training	

SECRET

WAR DIARY
3rd Bn Royal Fusiliers

OCTOBER 1918

3 Appendices

WAR DIARY or INTELLIGENCE SUMMARY.

Army Form C. 2118.

3 Royal Fusiliers

Place	Date	Hour	Summary of Events and Information	Remarks and references to Appendices
Battle Hqrs NURLU Sh57c.Q.30.c.50.50 Bn Ord D4.C.6.6. Bn Hqrs MONTBREHAIN B.10.a.40.60 Sh.51.b.55	Oct 1		Bn remained in billets during the morning. Midday received orders to relieve 8th Berkshire Regt in trenches (map ref. MONTBREHAIN. AP. 1M 1/20,000) Bn. Hqrs being at F.5. B.5.5. Bn distributed in platoon posts along front B50K.	[signatures] Officer in Adj 3rd Bde Officer on first line Adjutant 3rd Bde Hqrs
	Oct 2		Bn remained in trenches very quiet day. no casualties.	
	Oct 3		Bn still remained in trenches during morning & afternoon. Our Artillery bombarded enemy line heavily. At 1900 hrs Bn received orders to move to BONY POINT (REF MONT BREHAIN A 10.B. 7.3.) marching all night.	
MONTBREHAIN to BONY	Oct 4		Bn ordered to attack, Zero hour 0650 hrs. Jumping off line had moved into East. Northern portion of A 10.a. Objective was to be south of RICHARDS COPSE S.25.5. Objective was reached at 0730 hrs. Bn came under very heavy M.G. fire from LE CATELET BOULEVARD and received many casualties. Moving L Battalion on our flank not being successful the Bn had to withdraw to vicinity of jumping off line. The operation in itself was very successful about 300 enemy supply machine guns and some prisoners, despite the fact that the Bn. had to withdraw. The enemy had suffered up to such an extent to our fire, fell back to this form occupying trenches running from N.E. to S.W. in advance of Le Cateau ground being...	

Army Form C. 2118.

WAR DIARY
or
INTELLIGENCE SUMMARY.
(Erase heading not required.)

3 Royal Fusiliers

Place	Date	Hour	Summary of Events and Information	Remarks and references to Appendices
MONTREHAIN S. 28 1A.(Report)			Evening, with very few casualties indeed. Our casualties were 9 Officers killed, 2 Officers wounded, 32 OR. killed, 103 wounded, 4 missing. Officers killed were:- Lieut RH Micklem DSO Capt. RTFG Chadwick " Jm. McLaggan MC. RAMC. Capt/Adjt. WT Humphries Lieut PB Nepean " RAL Davies " REP Spies " BJ O'Connor Pharm H. March S/Lieut RDT Wolfe 2Lieut JM Smith. Officers wounded were:- Bn. was relieved by 150th BN. They concentrated at MAY COPSE (F9.C.7.5.) resting in the trenches round the Copse all the 5th. For four shells of a calf. G/Officer Lieut B Ball acting s/Adjutant. 3rd Royal Fusiliers	G/Officer an Lieut. s/(Adjutant) 3rd Royal Fusiliers
NEUF BERQUIN 28 1A. G100		0930	L.R. Bn. Comdr. Command of Lieut Tomms received orders to march to LA PANNERIE SOUTH (S9. B.5.5.)	
		17.15	Got further orders were issued to move on to VAUXHALL QUARRY (T25 a 6.10)	

Army Form C. 2118.

WAR DIARY
or
INTELLIGENCE SUMMARY.
(Erase heading not required.)

3 Royal Fusiliers

Instructions regarding War Diaries and Intelligence Summaries are contained in F. S. Regs., Part II. and the Staff Manual respectively. Title pages will be prepared in manuscript.

Place	Date	Hour	Summary of Events and Information	Remarks and references to Appendices
Bn HQ TRENCHES VAUCELLES DIARY.	Oct 7.		Ord to occupy trenches west of Quarry. Bn. remained there over night, & were heavily shelled. Major W.L. Trevenen joined & took over Battalion. In the afternoon orders were received to relieve Sherwood Foresters at GUISANCOURT FARM (T29.c.4.0) 2nd Dublins on our left were fighting for VILLERS FARM (T20.d.7.7) Scottish Horse were holding MASNIÈRES BEAUREVOIR LINE N. & S. of kind Guisancourt farm.	"Reinf": 3rd Royl Fus. "Adjt": 3rd Royl Fus.
EN HQ GUISANCOURT 8 FARM T29.C.4.0	Oct 8.		Bn was relieved in the early morning by Gloucester Regt. (4th Div.) The Bn. on passing through Bn. and passing along line of Railway Line back. Bn. remained at Guisancourt Farm. Bn. acting also at Guisancourt Farm. Bn received orders to move (preceded by Bn. E. MARETZ) (nr. Reims DU 1570 V.600 U.6.D) & marched to MAUROIS (P.2.3)	"Adjt" 3rd Royl Fus. "Adjt" 3rd Royl Fus.
BN HQ MAUROIS P.22.B REF. FRANCE SHEET57B	Oct 11		All of it was killed, the civilian population still being this village. Lieut L.P. Niman from our draft of 4 Augt. Orders were received to stand by ready to move at one hours notice.	"Reinf" 3rd Royl Fus.

Army Form C. 2118.

WAR DIARY
or
INTELLIGENCE SUMMARY.
(Erase heading not required.)

3rd Royal Fus.

Place	Date	Hour	Summary of Events and Information	Remarks and references to Appendices
BN. HQ. MAUROIS	Oct 12		Battle surplus rejoined, including the following Officers:— Capt Gorton, Lieuts Turner, Morris, – Forster, Bean, – Large, Long, – Bailhache, Sweetman, – Parry, Lieut. Bn. moved from MAUROIS to adjoining village HONNECHY	2/Lieutenant Quinn an. Lieut. & Adjutant 3rd Regt. Hussian.
BN HQ HONNECHY	Oct 13		Bn. remained in readiness to move at short notice, being Battalion on duty in Bde.	2/Lieutenant Quinn an. Lieut. (Adjutant) 3rd Regt. Hussian Company Imed.
	Oct 14		Bn. still in Billets at HONNECHY. Companies at disposal of Company imed. Lieut-Col M.O. Clarke, DSO joined & took over Command of Bn. Bn. strength 28 Officers 476 O.R.	
BN. HQ. HONNECHY	Oct 15		Bn. still in Billets. Preparing for pending operation.	2/Lieutenant Quinn an. Lieut. (Adjutant) 3rd Regt. Hussian
	Oct 16		Companies training under Company arrangements.	

WAR DIARY or INTELLIGENCE SUMMARY

Army Form C. 2118.

3rd Royal Fusiliers.

Place	Date	Hour	Summary of Events and Information	Remarks and references to Appendices
Map Ref. Sheet 57B 1/40,000	Oct 19		The Bn. left Billets in Honnechy at 0300 hrs & proceeded to Assembly Point Q.27.a.5.6. to take part in Divisional Operations. The enemy were holding the line of the Railway which runs parallel to the River Selle and advanced posts in the Eastern portion of Le Cateau, & between the Railway & river as far south as St Souplet. Account of Bn. fighting, Operation orders, also map attached. Bn. was commanded by Major Toovenitor. Strength going in to action 11 Off & 308 O.R. Our casualties were 1 Off missing & wounded. 2 Lieut. Regel missing. 2 Lieut. Forster wounded O.R. { 10 missing 67 wounded, 8 killed 8 gassed Bn. came out of the line to rest billets at Honnechy early in the morning, moving in the afternoon into Maretz.	Bn. Operation orders. Bn. Special account with map.
Bn. HQ. Maretz France Sheet 57B 4.6.	Oct 19		Rested during the morning, moving in the afternoon into Maretz about 3 miles distance.	

Army Form C. 2118.

WAR DIARY
or
INTELLIGENCE SUMMARY.
(Erase heading not required.)

3rd Royal Fusiliers.

Place	Date	Hour	Summary of Events and Information	Remarks and references to Appendices
BN HQ MARETZ	20th Oct		Divisional Church parade in factory March.	
	21st		Companies at disposal of Coy. Comdrs. for inspections generally.	
	22nd		Brigade paraded in factory for inspection by G.O.C. Division who addressed the troops regarding the excellent work they had done during the past months operations. Lieut A.W. Howell joined Bn. on posting.	
	23rd		Company training.	
	24th		Companies paraded for G.O.'s inspection in the morning. Remainder of the day General Training under Company arrangement. Lieut. P.G. Wilson joined Bn. on posting.	
	25th		Company training. Major Tradewith M.C. that was command of the 2nd Royal Dublin Fusiliers.	
	26th		Draft of 206 men arrived as reinforcements. Company Trainer TD.	
	27th		Draft inspected by G.O.C. 149 Brigade at 08.30 hours. Brigade Church Parade in Theatre Maretz. 2 Lt T. Ogden appointed assistant Adjutant.	

Army Form C. 2118.

WAR DIARY
or
INTELLIGENCE SUMMARY.
(Erase heading not required.)

Instructions regarding War Diaries and Intelligence
Summaries are contained in F. S. Regs., Part II.
and the Staff Manual respectively. Title pages
will be prepared in manuscript.

Place	Date	Hour	Summary of Events and Information	Remarks and references to Appendices
Bn HQ MARETZ	28th		Company training in wood, fighting & smoke barrage in wood near Ensigny. Warning order to move in following day. TD	
	29th		At R.E. Prudhomy joined us from Depot. 2 Pr A.C.R. Palmer admitted to Hospital. Battalion left MARETZ & proceeded to billets in REUMONT marching across country. TD	
Bn HQ REUMONT	30th		Major Trenowler rejoined Battn from 2nd Royal Dublin marching Battalion (field state with Cadre in high ground between REUMONT & ST BENIN & proceeded to 1.19 to 50 N.W. of POMMEREUIL (Refce Map 57B 40,000) where they bivouaced for the night.	
Bn HQ 1.19 to 60 N.W. POMMEREUIL. Refce Map 57B			Battle Surplus moved up to billets in LE CATEAU. Battle Surplus consisted of Major Trenowler, 11 C. Capt. Godfrey Capt. Buckville Lt Turner, Lt Bobin, Lt Ogden, 2nd Lt Knight & 57 O.R.	
Bn HQ FORTIER AUBOIS	31st		Battalion relieved 7th Welch at dusk in the line N/B 1 & 4 Coys in the line No 3 in Support. No 2 in Reserve, line running through C8 & mid A. (Refce Map 57B 40,000) Strength 16 Battalion 26 Officers 584 O.R. 2 R.F.N. Other ranks wounded 1 O.R. killed 1 O.R. wounded in bringing up rations. TD	

Thomas Ogden 2nd Lt
Comdg 3 R.F.

SECRET   3rd Battalion Royal Fusiliers   Copy No. 2.
Order No. 2.

Ref. Sheet 57B 1/40,000.   In the Field
October 16, 1918.

The following orders are issued in confirmation of the verbal instructions given to Company Commanders, and lectures to all N.C.Os and men of the Battalion on the forthcoming operations.

1. The attack on the red dotted line (1st Objective) will be carried out by the 151 Infantry Brigade.

2. The attack on the red line (2nd Objective) will be carried out by the 149 Infantry Brigade, with three Battalions in the line:-
   3rd Royal Fusiliers on the Right.
   2nd Royal Dublin Fusiliers in the centre.
   Scottish Horse on the Left.

3. The 3rd Royal Fusiliers will move from HONNECHY at 0030 hours 17th October via the track through P.23.D central, cross road P.30.A, Q.19 central, Q.26.A.9.3, thence to Dry Nullah in Q.21.C.3.0, where the Battalion will be assembled by 0400 hours.
   The Scottish Horse will be on the right in the assembling area.

4. The Battalion will follow the Scottish Horse across the bridges over the SELLE at Q.28.B.0.3, and will concentrate about Y Nullah at Q.29.A.5.9
   Companies will cross in the order, Nos 1, 2, 3, 4.
   No.1 Company will be so disposed as to protect the right flank of the 151st I. Brigade.

5. Nos. 2, 3, & 4 companies will be formed up ready to cross the red dotted line at Zero plus 135 minutes.
   No.1 Company will move in support 200 yards in rear of Left Flank of No.2 Company.

6. No.2 Company will detail a Liaison Platoon to keep touch with the 27th American Division. A standing Liaison Post will be established at LA ROUX FARM as soon as the red line (2nd Objective) has been gained.

Order No. 2. (Page 2)

7. Inter-company boundaries have been issued to Company Commanders, and especial attention is called to the necessity of thoroughly cleaning up LE QUENNELET FARM, LA ROUX FARM, and the orchards in Q.18 D Q 24 A and B ; No 4 Company will be prepared to assist the 2nd Royal Dublin Fusiliers in "mopping-up" the orchard in Q 12 D should necessity arise.

8. The attack will be made under a barrage of 18 pounders, and heavy artillery. The barrage will move in lifts of 100 yards in 3 minutes.

9. Four Tanks (1, 2, 43 and 45) of "C" Company No 1. Tank Battalion will assist the Battalion in its advance. No 2 Tank will be specially told off to clear LE QUENNELET FARM and LA ROUX FARM and the intermediate orchards on the right flank.

10. Nos. 2, 3 and 4 Companies will consolidate in depth as soon as the RED LINE is gained.

 No 1 Company will be in support along the road in Q. 18 D, but must be prepared to throw out a defensive flank, should the Americans fail to reach the RED LINE.

11. Battalion Headquarters will be at Q 21 C. 3.0 until the Red dotted line is captured, when it will move to Y Nullah at Q 23 C. 5.0.

 A further move will be made to QUENNELET FARM when the RED LINE has been captured.

 The R.A.P. will be at or near Battalion Headquarters.

12. Four men per platoon of the leading wave will light flares on the RED LINE, when called for by contact aeroplanes, at ZERO plus 190 minutes, and ZERO plus 250 minutes. The remainder of the men will wave their helmets.

13.

Order No 2. (Page 3)

13. Prisoners of War will be sent to Battalion Headquarters, thence to Brigade Headquarters at Q 19 Central. An escort of 1 man to every 10 prisoners must be detailed and a receipt will be obtained for the prisoners when handed over to Brigade Headquarters. Receipts will be handed in to Battalion Headquarters.

14. 149 Brigade Headquarters will be at Farm Q.19 Central, at ZERO minus 60 minutes, and moves to Q.20.B.8.6 when the Red dotted line has been established — all reports for Brigade Headquarters to Q.19 Central until ZERO plus 135 minutes, after that to Q.20.B.8.6

15. Zero hour will be notified later.

Issued at 1800 hours.

C. Turman, Lieutenant.
A/Adjutant, 3rd Bn Royal Fusiliers

Copy No. 1. Retained.
" " 2. War Diary ✓
" " 3. O.C. No. 1 Company
" " 4. " " 2 "
" " 5. " " 3 "
" " 6. " " 4 "
" " 7. 149 I. Brigade.
" " 8. Quartermaster.
" " 9. R.T.O.
" " 10. M.O.
" " 11. Signalling Officer.

SECRET

3rd Battalion Royal Fusiliers   Copy No.

Addenda to Order No. 2

In the Field   16th October 1918.

1. Immediately the Red Line is gained posts will be established 500 yds inclusive in advance of it. The 150th Infantry Brigade will pass through Red Line at Zero plus 6 hours.

2. Every other man will light flares on Red Line at Zero plus 190 minutes, and the remaining men who have not lighted flares will light them at Zero plus 250 minutes. This is particularly necessary in view of the bad weather which will necessitate aeroplanes flying very low unless flares are lighted in large numbers.

3. White Very Lights will be fired as the leading waves cross the Red Dotted Line and again when the Red Line is reached.

4. ZERO is 0520 hours.

5. Acknowledge.

Issued at 2015 hours.

                                                    Lieut.
                        A/Adjutant 3rd Battn. Royal Fusiliers

Copy No 1.   Retained
      2   War Diary
      3   O.C. No 1 Coy.
      4   "   " 2 "
      5   "   " 3 "
      6   "   " 4 "
      7   ~~HQ Brigade~~
      8   ~~Quartermaster~~
      9   ~~RTO~~
     10   ~~Medical Officer~~
     11   Signalling Officer

(6392) Wt. W6192/P875 1,500,000 4/18 McA & W Ltd (E 2815) Forms W3091/4.   Army Form W.3091.

H.7.C.
(61 sheets)

Cover for Documents.

Vol 6

~~Nature of Enclosures.~~

War Diary

3rd Battalion Royal Fusiliers

November - 1918

Appendices 13.
Maps   2.

Notes, or Letters written.

Army Form C. 2118.

WAR DIARY
or
INTELLIGENCE SUMMARY.
(Erase heading not required.)

3rd ROYAL FUSILIERS

Place	Date	Hour	Summary of Events and Information	Remarks and references to Appendices
Hight	Oct: 31/Nov 1st		The Battalion relieved the 7th Battalion the Wiltshire Regiment of the 150th Infantry Brigade, in the Right Subsector of the 50th Divisional front from G90.0.7 to G2D.5.3. The front consisted of a series of posts, organized in depth. A skeleton defence scheme was issued and all officers and N.C.Os were ordered to make themselves acquainted with the front occupied by No.1 Company, that being the front from which the Battalion would operate. Companies were ordered to carry out vigorous patrolling with a view to locating the enemy posts, and in order to keep enemy patrols clear of NO MANS LAND. The Brigade ordered no offensive action to be undertaken with a view to extending our line. A warning order was sent to companies that No.4 Company would be relieved by SCOTTISH HORSE tomorrow – Guides to be at Battalion Headquarters by 3 p.m.	Reference Sheet 57A.N.W.
	Nov: 1st	00.05 hrs	Enemy artillery very active with field guns and 4.2 howitzers, harassing village of FONTAINE-AU-BOIS and particularly the cross roads in L11D and G7B.	
	"	05.00 05.30 06.00	Very heavy fire on the village and about Battalion Headquarters – shelling of the forward area very slight. Most of the shells appeared to come from a N.E. direction. Dispositions of Battalion were as follows :– No.1 Company Right Company 10 Section Posts ⎱ Front Line. No.4 Company Left Company 6 Section Posts 1 Double Post Support 4 Section Posts Bn. Hdqrs. G7.B.3.0 Left Company Hqrs. G8.C.9.8 ⎱ N. of road Right Company Hqrs. G8.C.9.6	

Army Form C. 2118.

3rd ROYAL FUSILIERS

WAR DIARY or INTELLIGENCE SUMMARY.
(Erase heading not required.)

Place	Date	Hour	Summary of Events and Information	Remarks and references to Appendices
	Nov. 1st		Support Company 68.c.8.6 S. of road.	
			With 2 platoons N. of road in cellars 68.c.4.8	
			" 1 " S. " " " " " 8 " " "	
			" 1 " S. " " " " " 68.c.6.6.	
			Reserve Company N.W. of road in FONTAINE AU BOIS L.12.c.8.8.	
			The C.O. visited the companies in the Front Line, starting with No. 1 company on the right and visited each post in the line accompanied by Captain Large. A German post was located about G.9.a.2.6 and was sniped – the post appeared to consist of an officer and 6 or 7 men. After visiting the left post of our line, a gap of about 300 or 400 yards was found to exist between our left and the right of the Northumberland Fusiliers who had a post in the sunken road about G.2.D.45.30. Almost immediately S. of this post and in rear of it, was a house with some outhouses; in this the C.O. and Capt. Large located a party of Germans. Rallying up a few men fire was opened and the enemy compelled to retire into the building. Information was sent to the O.C. Right Company N.F., and the left platoon of No. 4 company was ordered to co-operate in dealing with the house. Owing however, to orders from higher authority that no offensive action was to be undertaken against the enemy, this house remained in possession of the enemy, and there is no doubt that he was able to watch our movements on the other side of the valley from this point and employed a machine gun to sweep the crest the next two days.	

Army Form C. 2118.

WAR DIARY
or
INTELLIGENCE SUMMARY.
(Erase heading not required.)

3RD ROYAL FUSILIERS

Place	Date	Hour	Summary of Events and Information	Remarks and references to Appendices
	Nov. 1st	11.00	L.O.C. 149th Inf. Brigade visited Bn. Hqrs; O.C. Scottish Horse came up and made arrangements to take over front held by left Coy (No. 4). Officers from the Tank Corps and 104 Bde R.F.A. came up and made arrangements for the operations on Nov. 4th. O.C. Tanks agreed to bring up tools and Lewis Gun ammunition for Battalion, and arrangements were made accordingly to deliver to them.	
	"	14.00	2/Lieut. H.D. Calder acting as Battalion Intelligence Officer returned to duty with No. 2 Company, and 2/Lieut. A.H. Bean took over the duties of Intelligence Officer. There being no Lewis Gun Officer at Battalion Headquarters, Lieut. H.S. Balding was sent up from Battle Surplus to undertake this duty and generally assist the Adjutant.	
	"	16.30	Enemy began to shell FONTAINE and continued till 17.00 hours, our artillery opened then and continued until 17.15". From that hour till 20.00 hours the front was quiet.	
	"	20.00	No. 4 Company relieved by one company Scottish Horse early in the evening and came into Support, remaining in cellars near their old Headquarters. Nos. 3 and 4 Companies were ordered to be prepared to reinforce any part of the Battalion front. The night passed comparatively quietly, but there was the usual shelling of tracks leading up to the Front Line. These tracks being now well defined and observed by hostile aeroplanes. Orders were issued to the Reserve Company to reconnoitre and use new lines of approach to the Front Line.	

Actual Casualties Oct: 31/Nov: 1st Killed. 1 O.R.
Wounded. 2/Lieut. F. Roberts and 1 O.R.

Army Form C. 2118

WAR DIARY
or
INTELLIGENCE SUMMARY

(Erase heading not required.)

3RD ROYAL FUSILIERS

Instructions regarding War Diaries and Intelligence Summaries are contained in F.S. Regs., Part II. and the Staff Manual respectively. Title Pages will be prepared in manuscript.

Place	Date	Hour	Summary of Events and Information	Remarks and references to Appendices
	Nov. 2nd	0600	0600 hours. A heavy artillery bombardment by both sides was opened on our immediate right, and lasted for about 40 minutes.	
		0600 to 0700	Battn. Headquarters was shelled with gas shells, and shelling in front area was abnormally heavy, and slight increase of hostile machine gun fire.	
		0800	The C.O., Battn. Intelligence Officer, and Company Commanders reconnoitred the general line selected for the jumping off point, viz from G.8.B.3.0. to G.8.A.95.65. Fontz was observed by the enemy and machine gun fire was opened on them, and the ridge was traversed. The fire appeared to come from the direction of the House at G.2.D.4.5.	
		0930	C.O. attended conference at Brigade Hqrs at POMMEREUIL. The general plan of the operation was explained, the chief points being (1) A barrage at 100 yards in 6 minutes on the whole army front; (2) to conform with this barrage line our front posts would have to be withdrawn from 200 yards to 500 yards on 2 night; (3) The line of the barrage, and therefore the jumping off line would be oblique to our general line of advance, i.e. facing N.E., whereas our advance would be generally in an Easterly and S.E. direction. The frontage on which the Battalion would form up was approximately 350 yards.	Preliminary instruction No. 1 A Minute I
		12.15	The Divisional Commander called at Battalion Headquarters.	
		14.00	Battn. Headquarters moved to G.8.c.5.9. This was almost immediately heavily shelled.	
		16.00	C.O. held conference of Company Commanders and explained the general outline of the operations, and as much detail as was available.	
		1800	Enemy artillery very quiet during the night. No. 3 Company relieved No. 1 Company on right of the line. 3rd Royal Fusiliers Preliminary Instruction No I (Appendix No I) issued to Companies.	

Army Form C. 2118

WAR DIARY
or
INTELLIGENCE SUMMARY
(Erase heading not required.)

3RD ROYAL FUSILIERS

Instructions regarding War Diaries and Intelligence Summaries are contained in F. S. Regs., Part II. and the Staff Manual respectively. Title Pages will be prepared in manuscript.

Place	Date	Hour	Summary of Events and Information	Remarks and references to Appendices
	Nov. 2 1918	22.00 hrs.	149th Brigade Preliminary Instructions No.1 Series A. received.	Appendix 2.
	Nov. 3 1918	03.00 hrs.	No. 3 Company reported enemy using RED ground flares, and hostile artillery much more active, thoroughly searching the ground round our front line, and particularly so in the neighbourhood of the forming-up line and to the East of it. A heavy ground mist.	
		09.00 hrs.	The C.O. visited Headquarters of 8th Royal Warwicks on right and ascertained that the Posts in the WHITE HOUSE at G9.c.3.3 had been strengthened, and that a line of posts had been established on the line G9.0.1.2, G8.D.9.0, G14.B.7.8, and thence to G.14 central. There was no question of a German withdrawal. This advance made our right flank much more secure.	
		12.00 hrs.	Company Commanders conference.	
		12.10	Battalion Headquarters heavily shelled with Gas shell and H.E.	
		14.00	Addendum No.1 to 149th Brigade Instructions No.1 received.	Appendix 3.
		14.10	Preliminary Instruction No.2 issued to companies.	Appendix 4.
		16.00	The C.O. visited No.1 Company Headquarters and No.3 Company and then went down the Taped Jumping-off Line with the Brigade Intelligence Officer and R.E. Officer. Hostile artillery was searching this area and obviously had the line well registered.	
		17.10	149th Inf. Brigade Order No.56 received.	
		18.00	3rd Royal Fusiliers Operation Order No.4 issued to companies.	Appendix 5.
		19.40	Tanks were ordered to be formed up 400 yards behind the infantry at Zero minus 1 hour.	Appendix 6.
		19.45	Headquarters and area shelled with gas shells.	

Army Form C. 2118.

WAR DIARY
or
INTELLIGENCE SUMMARY.
(Erase heading not required.)

3RD ROYAL FUSILIERS

Instructions regarding War Diaries and Intelligence Summaries are contained in F. S. Regs., Part II. and the Staff Manual respectively. Title pages will be prepared in manuscript.

Place	Date	Hour	Summary of Events and Information	Remarks and references to Appendices
	Nov. 3rd	22.00	L.O.C. 149th Inf. Brigade visited Battalion Headquarters.	
	Nov. 3/4		Night comparatively quiet in forward area - considerable shelling in back areas.	
	Nov. 4	05.25	No. 1 Company reported in position - Captain MURRAY LARGE reported killed by shellfire, and half of No. 1 Platoon casualties on tape line.	
		05.25	No. 3 Company reported in position.	
		05.25	No. 4 Company reported in position.	
		05.30	No. 2 Company reported in position.	
		05.35	Reported to 149 Infy Brigade :- "Companies in position, and enemy have the line of the Tape and are firing in enfilade from the S.E." The barrage of the Division on our right having opened at 05.45 hours provoked a very heavy barrage on our front area, especially in the vicinity of the Jumping-off line. The weather damp and misty, and our own barrage caused a thick fog, preventing one from seeing more than 20 or 30 yards.	
		05.45	The barrage on FONTAINE AU BOIS increased in intensity, especially along the roads and tracks leading up to the Jumping-off line.	
		06.15	Our barrage opened punctually - all communication was cut, all lines being down. Battalion Headquarters was heavily shelled with 5.9", 4.2", and gas shell.	

Army Form C. 2118.

WAR DIARY
or
INTELLIGENCE SUMMARY.
(Erase heading not required.)

3RD ROYAL FUSILIERS

Place	Date	Hour	Summary of Events and Information	Remarks and references to Appendices
	Nov 4	07.10	No information having been received either from companies, or from SCOTTISH HORSE on 8th Warwicks, runners were sent out to the two latter to obtain situation reports. The two runners sent to the SCOTTISH HORSE never returned.	
		08.15	Sent out 2/Lieut. Bean, Battalion Intelligence Officer, to get in touch with SCOTTISH HORSE and Lieut. Balding to get in touch with No. 2 Company	
		08.30	Pte Town from the left platoon of No. 4 Company reported at Headquarters with 9 prisoners belonging to the 86th Regiment and 153th Regiment captured about G.8.B.9.8; these men surrendered without much resistance. Tanks were reported doing good work, and troops reported about 500 yards across the road in G.9 Central. SCOTTISH HORSE however, reported their men as being held up at this spot at 07.45 hours. Casualties reported not very heavy after moving off and hostile artillery fire light. No. 4 Company was in touch with No. 1, but own men had not reached G.9.D by 08.00, according to Pte Town's report.	
		08.50	1/6th Royal Warwicks reported that walking wounded cases stated their troops had reached the line of the Light Railway running from G.15.B.9.9 to G.15.D.7.8.	
		09.00	No reports received either from Lieut. Balding or 2/Lieut. Bean. Barrage on road heavy and several casualties among runners.	

Army Form C. 2118.

WAR DIARY
or
INTELLIGENCE SUMMARY.
(Erase heading not required.)

3RD ROYAL FUSILIERS

Instructions regarding War Diaries and Intelligence Summaries are contained in F. S. Regs., Part II. and the Staff Manual respectively. Title pages will be prepared in manuscript.

Place	Date	Hour	Summary of Events and Information	Remarks and references to Appendices
	Nov. 4.	09.30	Lieut. Balding's servant returned, stating they had run into some shell fire; the officers and he had scattered and he could not find Lieut. Balding nor see any signs of 2/Lieut. Bean and his runner.	
		09.35	SCOTTISH HORSE reported their leading companies had crossed ROSIMBOIS Road at 09.00 hours and were in touch with our companies.	
		10.00	Lieut. Balding returned, having been wounded in the back (later it was discovered he had shrapnel in the stomach).	
		09.45	1/8th. Royal Warwicks reported that at 08.40 their right company had reached G.16.c.85.70. but were held up by machine guns in G.16.D. They had taken about 100 prisoners.	
		09.55	149th. Inf. Brigade message B.M. 660 received stating 150th Brigade making progress on left and success being exploited by 2 battalions of 151 Brigade who were moving up by the ROUTE de FONTAINE and LAIE du MONT CARMEL.	
		10.15	Moved Headquarters to G.9.A.3.2 and joined SCOTTISH HORSE there.	
		10.30	SCOTTISH HORSE reported their left company at DRILL GROUND CORNER and their right company at G.10.B.5.0 at 09.45 a.m. in touch with our left company.	
		10.45	A message received from 2/Lieut. Bean timed 10.25 hours stated he was in touch with D company of the SCOTTISH HORSE whose Headquarters were at G.9.B.1.8. - "B" company of this Battalion held up on line G.10.A.7.8 to G.10.A.5.6. - Reinforced by Support company "C".	

me

Army Form C. 2118.

WAR DIARY
or
INTELLIGENCE SUMMARY.

(Erase heading not required.)

Instructions regarding War Diaries and Intelligence Summaries are contained in F. S. Regs., Part II. and the Staff Manual respectively. Title pages will be prepared in manuscript.

3RD ROYAL FUSILIERS

Place	Date	Hour	Summary of Events and Information	Remarks and references to Appendices
	Nov. 4	11.45.	Scottish Horse reported approaching HAUTE CORNÉE at 11.00 hours.	
		11.50	Telephone message from Brigade Major saying the Bosche on the run and units are to push on.	
		12.00 noon.	O.C. No.1 Company, 2/Lieut. Savours, reported objectives gained and consolidation being carried out on RED LINE – In touch with Warwicks on right and No.4 company on left – Casualties 1 Officer (killed) and 35 other ranks – timed 11.20 hours.	
		12.00 noon.	Message timed 11.30 hours from O.C. No.2 Company (Lieut. Tanner) reports "RED LINE reached – No.3 Company on Left – No.2 Company Centre & No.1 Company on Right – No.2 Company holds line G.11.D.5.5.	
			Later a message was received from O.C. No.3 Company (Lieut. Piedney) timed 13.45 hours, stated "The Battalion reached its objective at 10.10 hours – We are consolidating – In touch with SCOTTISH HORSE on our left and the WARWICKS on our right– We have captured a battery of Field Artillery complete with horses and limbers."	
			This message was not understood owing to the difference in timing (1 hr 20 minutes) with the other companies.	
			The RED LINE objective ran from the Railway N. of LANDRECIES G.18.A.0.5 through G.11.D.5.5 to G.11.D.3.8 (right of SCOTTISH HORSE) thence Northwards to the HAUTE CORNÉE Saw Mills.	

Army Form C. 2118.

WAR DIARY
or
INTELLIGENCE SUMMARY.
(Erase heading not required.)

3RD ROYAL FUSILIERS

Instructions regarding War Diaries and Intelligence Summaries are contained in F. S. Regs., Part II. and the Staff Manual respectively. Title pages will be prepared in manuscript.

Place	Date	Hour	Summary of Events and Information	Remarks and references to Appendices
	Nov. 4.	12.25	The Brigade having ordered the Battalion to occupy the belt of trees in G11B and G12 Central and the spur in G12D, an order was sent to O.C. No.2 Company to push on and carry out this operation as soon as possible with all the DUBLIN FUSILIERS available – the above line to become the final objective of the Royal Fusiliers. The SCOTTISH HORSE to be responsible for clearing the belt of trees from G11B.3.7 to the track in G12.A.3.5 – 3rd ROYAL FUSILIERS to G12 Central – ROYAL DUBLIN FUSILIERS to clear the spur from G12 Central to G12.D.9.5. These orders were addressed to O.C. No.2 Company.	Appendix 7.
		12.30	Headquarters moved by the ROSIMBOIS – LANDRECIES road to G10 A.7.3. The C.O. and Battalion Intelligence Officer (2/Lieut. Ream) pushed down the track running through G10B and G11C and visited the companies in the line, beginning on the right by the railway at G11B.7.9. Found No.2 company and Royal Dublin Fusiliers (about ½ a company) preparing to push on to the spur G12D and clear the belt of trees in G12C and A. companies were generally holding the line of the RED LINE and slightly in advance of it.	
		15.00	No.4 Company was much reduced in strength. Four Field Guns } were captured in G11C Three Machine Guns } Six Field Guns Two Machine Guns } were captured in G11D Ten Wagons Twenty Horses } by No.4 and No.2. companies.	

M²

Army Form C. 2118.

WAR DIARY
or
INTELLIGENCE SUMMARY.
(Erase heading not required.)

3RD ROYAL FUSILIERS

Place	Date	Hour	Summary of Events and Information	Remarks and references to Appendices
	Nov. 4		The following account of the action was given by the four company commanders. It was difficult to get them to agree on the subject of times and positions :-	

The Attack - FONTAINE AU BOIS, 4th November, 1918.

Reference Map :- 57.A. NW 1/20,000.

Formation   4   3   1
                        2

Zero :- 6.15 a.m.

Owing to the heavy mist which prevailed connection was lost almost immediately between the two leading companies, with the result that the support company reinforced the centre of the front line at 6.9.A.3.2. Here the Scottish Horse were held up by heavy machine gun fire and it was impossible for us to continue the advance. About 15 minutes later, when this opposition had been disposed of, the whole Brigade pushed forward and continued to meet with machine gun posts which were effectively dealt with.

On reaching the ROSIMBOIS Road, we again had to wait for the Scottish Horse to come up on our left. In the meantime we mopped up several houses in the vicinity and captured 20 prisoners. The Scottish Horse having come up, and being in touch with the Warwicks on our right, we again advanced and pressed closely upon the enemy who at this point were putting up a stubborn resistance. They eventually retired and left behind at L.11.6. four Field Guns and other Machine Guns

Army Form C. 2118.

WAR DIARY
or
INTELLIGENCE SUMMARY

(Erase heading not required.)

3RD. ROYAL FUSILIERS

Place	Date	Hour	Summary of Events and Information	Remarks and references to Appendices
	Nov. 4.		Company Commanders report (continued):- We then pushed on to the village of LES ETOQUIES, mopped it up, and then advanced to the RED LINE. The Reserve Company (No. 2) having reinforced the Left Company captured six Field Guns, two Machine Guns and Transport consisting of 20 horses, 10 wagons with baggage, together with 10 prisoners. We thus gained our objective at 11.30 hours and consolidated our position.	
			At 16.00 hours No. 2 Company held an outpost line along the belt of trees in G.12.A."	
		16.00	No. 2 Company now held the Outpost Line.	
		17.00	C.O. and Intelligence Officer returned and established Headquarters at G.16.4.9. C.O. and Brigade Major rode back to see the General, but he could not be found. It was considered of the utmost importance to seize the crossings and establish Bridgeheads at LE PONTONNIER (H.13.A.3.4) and HYDRAULIC RAM (H.7.B.2.0). The Royal Dublin Fusiliers were ordered to do this.	
		18.00	2/Lieut. Bean was sent forward to explain situation to O.C. No. 2 Company and order him to seize the HYDRAULIC RAM crossing, and establish a Bridgehead should the Royal Dublin Fusiliers fail to do so. Also to order No. 3. Company to move up in close support to No. 2, and occupy a line of high ground in G.12.C.	
		19.05	Battalion Orders issued to all companies	Appendix 8.
			A wet and windy night.	

WAR DIARY
or
INTELLIGENCE SUMMARY.
(Erase heading not required.)

Army Form C. 2118.

3RD ROYAL FUSILIERS

Place	Date	Hour	Summary of Events and Information	Remarks and references to Appendices
	Nov 4th 1918		Transport work – Nov 4th.	

Early in the morning two mules were killed by shell fire at POMMEREUIL, where the Transport lines were then located, while in a limber taking birds to be loaded on a Supply Tank. These birds were eventually got to the Tank Corps and were loaded on the Supply Tank for transport to the Battalion.

One hour after Zero a Battalion Refilling Dump was established in a farm at FONTAINE AU BOIS under Corporal Bryan. In taking up the first limber loads of ammunition, etc. for this dump, three of the Transport staff were wounded by shrapnel fire.

Orders to move Transport and Quartermaster's Stores were issued at midday and the move to FONTAINE AU BOIS was completed during the afternoon. Transport lines were established at the Refilling Dump.

Until midday, FONTAINE AU BOIS was under fairly heavy shell fire.

Hot soup was taken up to the Battalion on pack mules at 19.00 hours, and rations which had been delayed owing to the late arrival of the Supply Train, were taken up on limbers at about 01.00 hours, together with water. Owing to the bad state of the roads, and blocks caused by artillery which was moving up, each journey took about 6 or 7 hours.

Casualties November 4th, 1918:–
Killed, Capt. R.M. LARGE and 7 O.R.
Wounded, Lieut. H.S. BADING } and 102 O.R.
D.S. CORBETT }
P.E. WILSON
Missing, 7 O.R.

Army Form C. 2118.

WAR DIARY
or
INTELLIGENCE SUMMARY.
(Erase heading not required.)

3rd ROYAL FUSILIERS

Place	Date	Hour	Summary of Events and Information	Remarks and references to Appendices
	Nov 5th 1918.	02.00 02.30 hrs.	149th Inf. Brigade Order No. 58 received, ordering move for next day. 3rd Royal Fusiliers Order No. 5 issued.	Appendix 1.
		07.05	Starting point reached at SAW MILLS.	
		09.00	Rain started.	
		11.15.	Moved companies into SAW MILLS under such shelter as they provided.	
		13.00.	149th Inf. Brigade Order No. 59 received, ordering move at 14.00 hours to HACHETTE FARM. Order of march :- Scottish Horse 14.00 hours. 3rd Royal Fusiliers 14.10 hours. 149 French Mortar Battery 14.20 hours. Brigade Headquarters 14.25 hours. The Scottish Horse were late and marched one company in rear of 3rd Royal Fusiliers. Route :- Route de LANDRECIES to Point 135 - B.25.B.1.2 Cross Road B.20.c.8.4. The afternoon was very wet and the going very bad, delay being caused at two places where the road had been blown up - e.g. near Point 135 where a deviation had to be used; this was so bad that timbers had to be untended and carts sent round empty.	
		17.00	Battalion reached HACHETTE FARM, B.27.a.7.8. and occupied wooden buildings in vicinity of FARM, sharing these with the SCOTTISH HORSE and 149th Inf. Brigade. The buildings leaked badly, but there was plenty of straw and several good stoves which helped to dry wet clothes.	

Army Form C. 2118.

WAR DIARY
or
INTELLIGENCE SUMMARY.
(Erase heading not required.)

Instructions regarding War Diaries and Intelligence Summaries are contained in F. S. Regs., Part II. and the Staff Manual respectively. Title pages will be prepared in manuscript.

3RD ROYAL FUSILIERS

Place	Date	Hour	Summary of Events and Information	Remarks and references to Appendices
	Nov. 5th	20.00	Brigadier General Robinson held a conference and explained proposed operations for next day. It was originally proposed that the whole Brigade should advance on LEVAL at 4 a.m. next morning; this was subsequently modified in 149 Brigade Order No. 60 received at	
		23.00	A special company of the Scottish Horse consisting of 3 officers and 100 men were to reach point C.13.D.0.8 simultaneously with the passing of the HELPE River by the 150th Brigade, and then advance to the spur in C.160. At 07.00 hours the remainder of the 149th Inf. Brigade to cross Canal Bridge B17.D05.80, 3rd Royal Fusiliers leading and move via Road Junction B11.C.1.6 – Rue des HAIES Hts NOYELLES – to the position gained by the Scottish Horse. Thence to attack LEVAL and advance due East to the BROWN LINE, with right on road D.19.B.55 and left on Divisional Boundary D.19.0.0; 3rd Royal Fusiliers on right, Scottish Horse on left (this was actually reversed next day) and 2nd Royal Dublin Fusiliers in Brigade Reserve. 1 Section R.F.A and 1 Section Machine Gun Battalion to each Battalion. Owing to the non arrival of rations, only those men with 3 am rations were to be allowed to take part in the operations.	
		23.30	Company Commanders were told situation, proposals, and orders for next day – written orders to be issued later. Orders to move Transport at 0800 hours had been received but were cancelled, and we were ordered to stand by until 14.00 hours. Orders were subsequently received that Transport would remain at FONTAINE au BOIS until the following day.	

Army Form C. 2118.

3RD ROYAL FUSILIERS

WAR DIARY
or
INTELLIGENCE SUMMARY.
(Erase heading not required.)

Instructions regarding War Diaries and Intelligence Summaries are contained in F. S. Regs, Part II. and the Staff Manual respectively. Title pages will be prepared in manuscript.

Place	Date	Hour	Summary of Events and Information	Remarks and references to Appendices
	Nov. 5.		Rations, which were again very late owing to the Supply Train being delayed, together with hot soup, were taken up by limber. Owing to the roads near HACHETTE being blocked with traffic, limbers were not able to get along the road and near HACHETTE the rations had to be unloaded and put on pack mules. Owing to the congestion of traffic the transport was unable to return until the following morning, the night being spent in the open. Orders were received at 0500 hours for the whole of A and B Echelons to join the Battalion at HAUTE CORNEE. The Lewis Gun limbers did not rejoin the Transport until the close of the operations. Officers chargers were also sent up and remained with the Battalion. On the morning of this day two limber loads of ammunition and stores were taken up to the Battalion and on the return journey met a salvage party from the Battle Surplus and brought in several Lewis Guns and other salvaged material.	

Army Form C. 2118.

WAR DIARY
or
INTELLIGENCE SUMMARY.
(Erase heading not required.)

Instructions regarding War Diaries and Intelligence Summaries are contained in F. S. Regs., Part II. and the Staff Manual respectively. Title pages will be prepared in manuscript.

3RD ROYAL FUSILIERS

Place	Date	Hour	Summary of Events and Information	Remarks and references to Appendices
	Nov.6. 1918.	04.30	No rations yet received - Deficiency of 37 Iron Rations made up by SCOTTISH HORSE.	
		05.00	3rd Royal Fusiliers Order No.6 issued.	Appendix 1.
		05.30	Rations arrived.	
		07.00	Battalion moved off with No.2 leading, in column of route. Some shelling about the RUE du FNIX	
		08.30	Ordered to ride forward and meet Brigadier with Colonel Blair (S.H.) in BASSE NOYELLES.	
		09.00	Ordered by B.O.C. 149th Brigade to proceed up road to NOYELLES and cross River HELPE either by wading or by crossing over temporary bridge. Thence to advance and attack LEVAL. The Royal MUNSTER FUSILIERS were reported to have reached the Cross Roads in G21A at 07.30 hours.	
		10.00	Companies, which had concentrated in field S of BASSE NOYELLES, were ordered to push on and cross river by temporary bridge made of carts at NOYELLES.	
		11.28	Following message was sent to O.C. No.2 Company :- "33rd Division has pushed into LEVAL and went on to connect up with them as soon as possible and advance on to the BROWN LINE (CHAUSSÉE BRUNHAUT). Push out on to the Spur in O18A and get this to bear on LEVAL and push out the Bosche. Scottish Horse will be on your right and No.1. Company will support you closely."	
		12.00	Further message to No.2. Company to push on. C.O. with one runner and 2 or 3 men from Reserve Company (No.3) went forward.	Appendix 2.

Army Form C. 2118.

WAR DIARY
or
INTELLIGENCE SUMMARY.
(Erase heading not required.)

3RD ROYAL FUSILIERS

Instructions regarding War Diaries and Intelligence Summaries are contained in F. S. Regs., Part II. and the Staff Manual respectively. Title pages will be prepared in manuscript.

Place	Date	Hour	Summary of Events and Information	Remarks and references to Appendices
	Nov. 6.		Found Nos. 1 and 2 Companies about C.16.B.2.1. No.1 Company was ordered to push down into LEVAL and get in touch with 33rd Division, and the whole to advance with	
		1300	SCOTTISH HORSE on right. This advance was to be carried out as soon as No.1 Company was in position.	
PETIT LANDRECIES C.15.D.5.8.		14:00	The acting Adjutant (Captain Parker) and Battalion Intelligence Officer (2/Lieut Bean) having become casualties from shell fire, the C.O. on his return took Lieut. Sudney from No.3 Company as adjutant, leaving 2/Lieut Gowers in charge of this Company.	
		14:10	The Divisional Commander (General Jackson) arrived and ordered 3rd Royal Fusiliers and Scottish Horse to push on at once and endeavour to reach BROWN LINE before dark.	
		14:15	C.O. ordered 2/Lieut. Gowers to push through LEVAL by NORTHERN Road to Railway, and joining up with Nos.1 and 2 Companies to advance to the BROWN LINE.	
		14:20	C.O., Adjutant, and Signallers pushed on behind Companies to Railway Bridge C.11.C.2.5. - crossing very difficult owing to demolition, and much water on Eastern side owing to flooding of LA TARSY stream. A good deal of hostile machine gun fire on the right and some heavy shelling in LEVAL.	

Army Form C. 2118.

WAR DIARY
or
INTELLIGENCE SUMMARY.
(Erase heading not required.)

Instructions regarding War Diaries and Intelligence Summaries are contained in F. S. Regs., Part II. and the Staff Manual respectively. Title pages will be prepared in manuscript.

3RD ROYAL FUSILIERS

Place	Date	Hour	Summary of Events and Information	Remarks and references to Appendices
	Nov. 6	14.30	Battalion reached PETIT MAUBEUGE – ST WAAST Road without much opposition. Scottish Horse on right, 33rd Division on the left. On advancing to the BROWN LINE – road in C12B and D strong opposition was encountered, especially on the right flank. By dusk the two left companies had reached their objective.	
		16.00		
C11D.9.3.		16.30	Battalion Headquarters established at C11D.9.3. – 2/Lieut. Golden appeared with 2 men and stated No. 2 Company's right flank was in the air and no touch with the SCOTTISH HORSE, and a gap on their left, also they were running short of ammunition and required more at once.	
		16.45	As men of WORCESTERS had reported 33rd Division had not gone forward, and SCOTTISH HORSE were out of touch, Lieut. Sidney was sent back to Brigade to report position and bring up ammunition mules. A box of ammunition was obtained from the Machine Gun Company and sent forward.	
		17.00	2/Lieuts. Golden and C.O. and Lieut. Young the Brigade Intelligence Officer, went up to No. 2 Company and found this company was NOT on the BROWN LINE but on the ROMBISE – CORBEAU Road C12.D.0.5. Moving up the line to the left it was found a gap of 500 or 600 yards existed between No. 2 Company's left and No. 3 Company's right, while moving along road to No. 3 Company 2 Germans (fully equipped) were encountered by party and made prisoners. They seemed very surprised and screamed with fright.	

Army Form C. 2118.

WAR DIARY
or
INTELLIGENCE SUMMARY
(Erase heading not required.)

3RD ROYAL FUSILIERS

Place	Date	Hour	Summary of Events and Information	Remarks and references to Appendices
	Nov. 6. 1918.		The Transport and Quartermaster's Stores moved from FONTAINE AU BOIS to MAROILLES at 0900 hours, owing to the bad condition of the roads and to the fact that the bridge over the Canal at HACHETTE FARM had been demolished by the enemy. Progress on the roads was very slow. Rations were taken up this night on pack animals as it was impossible to get limbers along the roads. A start was made at about 1800 hours and the party did not arrive back until 0630 hours next morning. Hot soup was also taken up with the rations. There was considerable difficulty in finding the way as guides were not picked up and the Railway embankment at LEVAL had been blown up, necessitating a long detour. Many of the roads were flooded, and damaged by mine craters and shell fire, and a bridge over the river near NOYELLES had been demolished by the enemy. Casualties November 6th 1918. Wounded. Lieut. (A/Captain) F. PARKER, Junior 3 O.R. 2/Lieut. A.H. BERN	

Army Form C. 2118.

WAR DIARY
or
INTELLIGENCE SUMMARY.
(Erase heading not required.)

3RD ROYAL FUSILIERS

Place	Date	Hour	Summary of Events and Information	Remarks and references to Appendices
	Nov. 6		No.3 and No 1 companies were found digging in about 200 yards East of the CHAUSSEE BRUNHAUT and in touch with 33rd Division.	
ROMBISE FARM.		17.45	No. 2. Company ordered to move forward, occupy a line in advance of above road and in prolongation of No. 3 Company, and to get touch with SCOTTISH HORSE on the right.	
		18.00	C.O. returned to Headquarters early on road and made Headquarters with SCOTTISH HORSE at ROMBISE FARM C.18.A.3.7.	Appendix 3
		18.30	Message R.F.8, sent to 149 Brigade giving position of companies.	
		19.15	Right Company established on BROWN LINE and in touch with SCOTTISH HORSE.	
			Very wet day and cold wet night – troops thoroughly exhausted after long advance. The night passed quietly; rations arrived up late, transport having had much difficulty in getting up.	
ROMBISE FARM	Nov. 6/7.			
	Nov 7	02.30	149th Inf Bde B.M. 702 received, saying 151 Brigade would pass through BROWN LINE next morning at 08.00 hours and advance to the line of the MAUBEUGE-AVESNES road. After 151 Brigade has passed through, 149 Brigade to concentrate about D.13.A. Cold wet morning.	
		08.00	Companies were ordered to close on the right of No. 2 Company near LE CARBEAU.	
		12.00	Companies remained in the open at above point until nearly midday, when permission was received to move into billets. Although barns had been prepared and were ready near ROMBISE FARM for the reception of companies, the Battalion was ordered to go into	

Army Form C. 2118.

WAR DIARY
or
INTELLIGENCE SUMMARY.
(Erase heading not required.)

3RD ROYAL FUSILIERS

Place	Date	Hour	Summary of Events and Information	Remarks and references to Appendices
	Nov. 7 (cont.)		Billets at the Western end of St. REMY-CHAUSSÉE. These were found either to be occupied by other units or to be uninhabitable.	
		14.00	Permission was obtained to billet the men in the land originally arranged for them.	
		15.40	Companies in billets at C.18.A.8.8 — C.18.A.3.1 ; Battn. Headquarters at C.18.A.2.5.	
		16.00	Message of congratulation received from Army Commander and Divisional Commander. Appendix 1.	
		20.30	B.M. 706 — warning order for move tomorrow received. Brigade to be prepared to move at ½ hours notice any time after 09.00 hours on 8th. Troops to remain fully dressed.
The following order was also received "If German Officer bearing flag of truce presents himself at any point of British front, he will be conducted to the nearest Divisional Headquarters and detained there pending instructions from G.H.Q." This was our first official intimation that German envoys were expected to arrive in the Allied Lines with a request for an armistice on terms to be granted by Marshal FOCH.	

Army Form C. 2118.

WAR DIARY
or
INTELLIGENCE SUMMARY.
(Erase heading not required).

3RD ROYAL FUSILIERS

Place	Date	Hour	Summary of Events and Information	Remarks and references to Appendices
	Nov 9 1918.		The Transport and Quartermaster's Stores remained at MAROILLES during the whole of this day, opportunity being taken of attending to and resting the animals which were getting in poor condition owing to incessant working. Two G.S. wagons were sent back to fetch blankets and greatcoats, which had been dumped at FONTAINE au BOIS owing to lack of transport facilities when the stores moved up. Rations were taken up by limbers, each limber with four mules as the roads were very heavy and much damaged by mines. A start was made about 1700 hours and the party arrived back at 02.00 hours.	

Army Form C. 2118.

WAR DIARY
or
INTELLIGENCE SUMMARY.
(Erase heading not required.)

3RD ROYAL FUSILIERS

Place	Date	Hour	Summary of Events and Information	Remarks and references to Appendices
	Nov. 8	10.00	149 Brigade conference at Headquarters of Scottish Horse at 10.00 hours; company commanders warned that Battalion would be moving about noon.	
		11.30	C.O. returned from conference and explained plan to company commanders. 149 Brigade on a 3 Battalion front to pass through 151 Inf Brigade and advance to the track running North and South through the Bois de BEUGNIES, pushing out patrols beyond the Eastern edge of the forest. There were many indications that the Bosche intended to retire on the night Nov 8/9. A feeble counter attack had been made by the enemy against the 151 Brigade; the hostile infantry had shown no desire to come on, and the chief fight had been put up by the enemy's machine gunners and artillery.	
		11.00	The line held by the 151 Brigade was the line of the AVESNES–MAUBEUGE Road, with the right and left flanks refused – the Division on the right having made progress slowly, but reported to be advancing now satisfactorily. Northern Boundary of Brigade attack – an East and West line through D.12 Central – E.7.8.9.10.11 Central. Royal Fusiliers Left Boundary, just north of DOURLERS–MONT DOURLERS road, thence due East through E.15.16.17 Central.	

Army Form C. 2118.

WAR DIARY
or
INTELLIGENCE SUMMARY.
(Erase heading not required.)

3RD ROYAL FUSILIERS

Place	Date	Hour	Summary of Events and Information	Remarks and references to Appendices
	Nov. 8		Royal Fusiliers Right boundary Ruins des HERQUETTES – HUITHAU inclusive – E22.23 Central.	
		12.00	The Battalion moved off, No 3 Company leading – No. 1 – No. 2. Attack to be carried out with No. 3 on right, No. 1 on left, No. 2 in Reserve.	
		14.00	C.O. rode on to conference with C.O.C. 151 Brigade at west end of St AUBIN. C.O. rode on to DOURLERS and found C.O. of INNISKILLING FUSILIERS with Headquarters at sunken Cross Roads D18.D.6.7. Large trees felled on road just south of DOURLERS. CHATEAU blocked by fallen trees. Hostile harassing shell fire down this road, in DOURLERS CHATEAU grounds and N of DOURLERS.	
		15.30	Companies formed up in sunken Road in E.13.C and began advance at 15.40 on verbal orders of C.O. who said it was imperative an advance should be made before dusk. Battalion Headquarters was temporarily established in same road as companies, and after advance had begun moved up to house at E.13.D.60.65. The advance of the Battalion was carried out under heavy machine gun fire and some fairly considerable shelling, which latter however soon decreased in volume. Machine Gun fire mostly came from direction of E.20 Central and hedges N. of it.	

Army Form C. 2118.

WAR DIARY
or
INTELLIGENCE SUMMARY.
(Erase heading not required.)

3RD ROYAL FUSILIERS

Place	Date	Hour	Summary of Events and Information	Remarks and references to Appendices
	Nov. 5	16.30	Following up the attack East of the AVESNES-MAUBEUGE Road, the C.O. found the right of the Battalion rested about E.14.D.0.0, leaving a considerable gap between our right and Scottish Horse. No.3 Company sent out a patrol down the SEMOUSIES Road to connect up. There was still considerable machine gun fire coming from the direction of the hedges just North of E.20 Central.	
		17.00	On returning to the MAUBEUGE road, a Platoon of the SCOTTISH HORSE was run into. They had a Lewis Gun firing from the road, presumably at the C.O. and his escort, as no one else was visible and the nearest Germans were at least 500 or 600 yards distant. This Platoon was directed on our left.	
		18.00	The Adjutant was now sent out to get the position of No.1 company and find out if connection had been established with the Dubbins who were reported in FOURNIES. About 17.00 a message had been received from the Dubbins asking us to come up on their flank as fast as possible.	
		17.30	A message from 149 Brigade reported situation on right as follows:- "Whole AVESNES-MAUBEUGE Road held - 198 Brigade on our right - Division on our right is on road through E.26.D and K.2.B". This latter was later on proved to be correct, the General line actually running from the junction of the MAUBEUGE and	

Army Form C. 2118.

WAR DIARY
or
INTELLIGENCE SUMMARY.
(Erase heading not required.)

3RD ROYAL FUSILIERS

Instructions regarding War Diaries and Intelligence Summaries are contained in F. S. Regs., Part II. and the Staff Manual respectively. Title pages will be prepared in manuscript.

Place	Date	Hour	Summary of Events and Information	Remarks and references to Appendices
SARS POTERIES	Nov. 8	17.30	roads along sunken road just West of SEMOUSIES to MONT DOURLERS - thence to FLOURSIES.	
		18.35	Sent message to Royal Dublin Fusiliers saying our 3 companies aligned along the road from E.14.A.6.0 - through road junction E.14.C.9.6 to E.20.C.8.8 - Left company ordered to get into touch with right of Royal Dublin Fusiliers, and asked latter to say where right post was.	
		19.20	Message received from Scottish Horse giving their line as E.26.C.0.5 - E.20.C.4.0 - E.20.A.7.D - E.20.A.4.3, and gradually working forward to make good SEMOUSIES where there was heavy machine gun fire.	
		19.25	Dublins ask us to post LIAISON post at "L" in MONT DOURLERS.	
		19.30	Order sent to No.1 company to do so at once, and to move forward and make good the road through E.14.D - Dublins patrolling this road southwards from FLOURSIES. Companies asked to state what ammunition and grenades required to complete. O.C. No.1 company reported through Lieut. PUDNEY that 2/Lieut. LETHERBY and his platoon had gone N of DOURLERS and were lost. Probably went off with Dublin Fusiliers.	
		19.30	No.1 company reported not yet in touch with Dublin Fusiliers.	

Army Form C. 2118.

WAR DIARY
or
INTELLIGENCE SUMMARY.
(Erase heading not required.)

3RD ROYAL FUSILIERS

Place	Date	Hour	Summary of Events and Information	Remarks and references to Appendices
	Nov 8.	19.45	149th Brigade C.697 received stating (1) Information from prisoners and sound of mines blowing up point to a retirement by enemy on a large scale commencing tomorrow (2) No advance to be made beyond Eastern edge of FORÊT de BEAULIEU. (3) Cyclists to be sent out to keep touch with enemy and report any withdrawal. (4) 12 men of 12th Lancers under an officer will patrol main road to SARS POTERIES forming Divisional Southern boundary.	
		20.10	Situation report R.F. 63 sent to 149th Brigade.	Appendix 1.
		20.30	R.F. 64 to No.1 Company, ordered to put out LIAISON POST at "Z" of MONT DOURLERS E14D.5.9 where Dublin Fusiliers also have a post – and to advance his to road running from E14D.5.9 to E14.D.0.0.	
		20.45	R.F. 65 to No.1 Company, repeating same order and stating Dublins had withdrawn Liaison Post as No.1 Company had fired on them. Dublins asked to re-establish post.	
		21.05	Inform Scottish Horse of position and say that our right is being extended to point where stream crosses road at E.20.c.6.8.	
		22.10	No.1 Company report lost Platoon under 2/Lieut. LETHERBY recovered by Patrol – sent his 2/Lt to gain touch with Dublin Fusiliers whose right flank reported to be at E15.A.2.8. Lt.1 Company going to advance his to road in E14.D.	

Army Form C. 2118.

WAR DIARY
or
INTELLIGENCE SUMMARY.
(Erase heading not required.)

3RD ROYAL FUSILIERS

Place	Date	Hour	Summary of Events and Information	Remarks and references to Appendices
	Nov 8. 1918.		Transport and Quartermaster's Stores moved to LEVAL during the morning. Orders were received that the Battle Surplus would join the Transport at LEVAL, and billets were fixed up for them. They did not however arrive that day. Rations and hot soup were taken up in limbers — each limber with four animals. On arrival at the Battalion Refilling Point at ST AUBIN on was found impossible to take limbers any further, as the road was blocked by felled trees and there was considerable shelling going on. Rations were re-packed and the limber mules fixed up with pack saddles for taking the rations up to the Battalion in the line. Considerable delay was occasioned by loss of guides. On this occasion the roads as far as the Refilling Point were quite good and the party got back soon after 6.00 hours. Casualties November 8th 1918. Killed 1 OR. Wounded 6 OR.	

Army Form C. 2118.

WAR DIARY
or
INTELLIGENCE SUMMARY.
(Erase heading not required.)

3RD ROYAL FUSILIERS

Place	Date	Hour	Summary of Events and Information	Remarks and references to Appendices
	Nov. 8	22.30	C.O. went with runner (Pte SCAMMELL) and Intelligence Officer Scottish Horse to visit Battalion Headquarters Scottish Horse at E19.D.95.75. Arranged with Lt. Colonel BLAIR to take over from his left platoon (2) on the road as far as forked roads junction E.20.A.65.10 and to push on gradually to line of resistance on Western Edge of Forest of BEUGNIES, and advance through Forest to final objective at dawn.	
		23.45	Then went down our line – arranged with Lieut. Tanner (O.C. No. 2) to take over Scottish Horse posts – found 2/Lieut. Gowers (O.C. No. 3) pushing out posts on E.14.D central – collected all company commanders and a few others at No. 1 company Headquarters (Farm House E.14.C.8.8) and ordered them to push out strong patrols down the roads leading to the Forest of BEUGNIES and as each was reported clear, to move their companies forward until established on the line of resistance on Western Edge of the Forest. No advance to be made through the Forest until dawn.	
	Nov. 9	00.15	Sent a message to Scottish Horse to say the above was being carried out.	
		00.30	C.O. returned to Battalion Headquarters E.13.D.65.70.	
			A message had been received at 23.00 hours saying Division on left continuing advance under a barrage at 06.15 hours.	
		01.30	Report on state of roads leading East sent to Brigade Headquarters.	

Army Form C. 2118.

WAR DIARY
or
INTELLIGENCE SUMMARY.
(Erase heading not required)

3RD ROYAL FUSILIERS

Instructions regarding War Diaries and Intelligence Summaries are contained in F. S. Regs., Part II. and the Staff Manual respectively. Title pages will be prepared in manuscript.

Place	Date	Hour	Summary of Events and Information	Remarks and references to Appendices
	Nov. 9	01.45	Scottish Horse report Germans have left SEYMOUSES and Scottish Horse now advancing to make good the village. Thereafter advance to be made to West edge of wood if no resistance encountered and Patrols push out through wood also. First bound road through E.27.72 central. Second bound, stream through E.27.79.95.95; Third bound, West edge of wood.	Appendix 2.
		02.00	R.F. 69 sent out to companies saying HUITHAU occupied by Scottish Horse, and to push on by bounds to West edge of Forest, etc., as already arranged.	Appendix 3.
		02.15	R.F. 68 sent to 149 Brigade giving position and intentions.	
		02.30	Report from O.C. No. 2 Company that Scottish Horse Patrol found HUITHAU unoccupied.	
		03.40	Reported to 149 Brigade "Confirmation of Telephone message AAA Patrols report they have reached Line of Resistance (approximately N and S good line E of squares E 9.15.21.27) and there are no signs of the enemy AAA Companies are now pushing forward.	
		05.00	The Acting Adjutant, Lieut. Pudney, and C.O's groom rode up to the FOREST OF BEVENIES and HUITHAU respectively, and on returning reported country clear of enemy. Patrols from centre company penetrated Eastern edge of wood. Patrols on left held up by machine gun fire.	
		05.50	O.C. No. 2 Company reported his company at E.21.B. East of HUITHAU and in touch with SCOTTISH HORSE, and pushing forward at dawn.	
		06.00	R.F. 72 sent to 149 Brigade	
		06.00	SCOTTISH HORSE report moving Battalion Headquarters to E.21.D.0.8.	
		06.20	3rd Royal Fusiliers Headquarters move to E.15.C.6.5. Adjutant and half signallers and	

Army Form C. 2118.

WAR DIARY
or
INTELLIGENCE SUMMARY.
(Erase heading not required.)

3RD ROYAL FUSILIERS.

Instructions regarding War Diaries and Intelligence Summaries are contained in F. S. Regs., Part II. and the Staff Manual respectively. Title pages will be prepared in manuscript.

Place	Date	Hour	Summary of Events and Information	Remarks and references to Appendices
	Nov. 9 1918	06.30	Mules go to F.21.B.3.2. S.O. and mounted orderly, and portion of signallers and ammunition mules moved up to LA SAVATE, E.17.D.1.1. Companies had established a line along track running N and S through FORET de BEUGNIES with patrols E. of Forest. Met with no resistance during advance except on left where No. 1. met hostile M.G. – No. 2. Right. No. 3 in centre – No. 2. Right. Companies were ordered to take up a line of outposts along line of road running N and S through LA SAVATE.	
		07.30	Found Cross Roads at LA SAVATE blown up. Met Divisional Commander who said Germans were in full retreat – revolution in BERLIN and in north sea ports – Kaiser abdicated, and end of war in sight.	
		10.00	149 Bde. B.M. 731 received, ordering Battalion to concentrate in billets in MONT DOURLERS after 150th Brigade had passed through our lines at LA SAVATE. Brigadier, however, ordered Battalion to at once commence work on deviation round crater on Cross Roads. Battalion worked until 13.15 hours, then marched to MONT DOURLERS.	
		15.00	Battalion went into billets in MONT DOURLERS, thoroughly exhausted with lack of sleep and exposure, but otherwise happy in feeling they had successfully fought their last battle in this great war.	

Army Form C. 2118

WAR DIARY or **INTELLIGENCE SUMMARY**
(Erase heading not required.)

3RD ROYAL FUSILIERS

Place	Date	Hour	Summary of Events and Information	Remarks and references to Appendices
	Nov. 9 1918.		Transport and Quartermaster's Stores moved to ST. AUBIN at 09.00 hours. During the afternoon at ST. AUBIN, orders were received to send 4 limbers to Brigade to form part of a Mobile Column for a force following up the enemy. These limbers were returned at night as the operation had been cancelled as far as it affected the 50th. Division. Blankets and Greatcoats were taken up to the Battalion in the afternoon and issued to the men. As the Battalion was in billets in MONT DOURLERS, no difficulties arose with rations this night. Lieut. NUNAN took over the Transport from 2/Lieut. OGDEN on arrival of the Battle Surplus at ST. AUBIN.	

Army Form C. 2118.

WAR DIARY
or
INTELLIGENCE SUMMARY.
(Erase heading not required.)

3rd Royal Inniskilling(?)

Place	Date	Hour	Summary of Events and Information	Remarks and references to Appendices
BN. H.Q. MONT DOURLERS	10 Nov 1918		Batth. in Billets in MONT DOURLERS. Battle Surplus rejoined consisting of Major Tranmate M.C. Capt Balhouie M.C. Capt Bathurst M.C., 2 Lt O'Neill, the following Officers who had joined the Battn. on paths; Capt E A W Hughes, 2Lt H.S. Murdoch M.C. 2 Lt C A W Hunt, 2 Lt G.H. McKernan, 2 Lt R.C. Maule, M/Capt A D Young C.F. Lt Numan rejoined from leave & took over the duties of Transport Officer.	
	11 Nov.		Notice from Brigade received to effect that an Armistice had been signed with Germany & that hostilities would cease at 0.11 hours on the 11th Nov. Coys engaged in internal economy & cleaning up Billets. Draft of 1 Officer (2/Lt Antigun) + 58 O.R. reported at 19.30 hours to Coys.	T.D.
	12 Nov.		Battn. in Billets in MONT DOURLERS. M.O. inspected new Drafts at 10 hours and men were allocated to Coys. Battn. paraded before the Divisional General at 10.30 hours who addressed the parade on the subject of the recent operations and, after a short Pinnell Service, presented medal ribbons to the following:- 15248 Sgt T Curry, 11936 Sgt. F. Weedon M.M., 11306 Pte A. Somerville, 18514 Pte F Wilson. Commander Officers read out on Parade the list of their Officers & O.R. killed in action during the recent operations.	T.D.
	13 Nov.		Draft inspected by the C.O. at 12.30 hours. Transport & Q.M. Stores paraded before the C.O. at 12.45 hours. Comdg officer inspected & addressed by him on the subject of the recent operations. Coys. carried on with their training according to the programme of work.	T.D.
	14 Nov.		Working parties consisting of No 1 & 2 Coys. under Major Tranmate proceeded to SARS POTERIE at 0.53 hours to work on indicating ammunition. Remainder of Battn. paraded before the C.O., who read out to them the terms of the Armistice after which Coys. carried on training as usual. Captain Hughes took over duties of Adjutant from Lieut Pinkerton, who took command of No 2 Coy. Capt. Young C.F. admitted to hospital.	T.D.
	15 Nov.		Working party, as before consisting of No 2 & 3 Coys under Major Tranmate proceeded to Sars Poterie to report there for work on indicating ammunition at 12 hours. Remainder of Battn. carried on with Coy. training. 2/Lt R. Stevenson joined the Battn. on posting.	T.D.

Army Form C. 2118.

WAR DIARY
INTELLIGENCE SUMMARY.
(Erase heading not required.)

Instructions regarding War Diaries and Intelligence Summaries are contained in F. S. Regs., Part II. and the Staff Manual respectively. Title pages will be prepared in manuscript.

3rd Royal Fusiliers

Place	Date	Hour	Summary of Events and Information	Remarks and references to Appendices
BN. H.Q. MONT DOURLERS	16 Novr. 1918		Working party as before reported to Sous Officer Rly. Station under Lt. Tarrant for work on ammunition dump. Party cancelled by Nos. 1,3,4 Corps and started work at 0.06 hours return to Billets after dinner. 149 Bde. R.T.M.B. was temporarily destroyed at 14.00 hours. 9 Other ranks rejoined the Battn. from the S.T.M.B. and were posted to their respective Companies after being inspected by the Adjutant.	
	17 Novr 1918		Working party of 1, 2 & 4 Coys as before. Remainder of Battn. attended a Church Parade in the open air at MONT DOURLERS. Captain Gordon rejoined the Battn. the Corps Commanders Course having been cancelled in expectation of hostilities.	
	18 Novr 1918		Battn. carried out training according to programme of work. No working parties. Lt. Hartloh left for England to Report to the War Office on a compassionate grant and in accordance with War Office instructions who struck S/S our strength.	
BN. H.Q. DOURLERS	19 Novr.		The Battn. moved into new Billets in DOURLERS. Nos. 2 & 4 Companies were engaged on Salvage work in the Area South of DOURLERS all salvaged ammunition and material being dumped on the Battn. Salvage Dump. The remaining three Companies carried out training as usual.	
	20 Novr.		Nos. 1 & 3 Coys Engaged on Salvage work. Nos. 2, 4 Coys on training. 2/Lt. E.R. BROWN joined the Battn. in hospital. 2 Lt. Seaman left on leave to England.	
	21 Novr.		Nos. 2 & 4 Coys on Salvage work. Nos. 1 & 3 Coys on training. A sports meeting of representatives from each Company was held at 14 hours.	
	22 Novr.		Nos. 1 & 3 Coys on Salvage work. Nos. 2 & 4 on training. The following Officers are joining the Battn. in posting. 2/Lt. Warden S.W. 2/Lt Ford J.H. 2/Lt Nill J.W. 2/Lt Turner W.E. 2/Lt. Rapto P. MM. 2/Lt Newton A.J. (Contd)	

Army Form C. 2118.

WAR DIARY
or
INTELLIGENCE SUMMARY.
(Erase heading not required.)

3rd Royal Fusiliers

Place	Date	Hour	Summary of Events and Information	Remarks and references to Appendices
BN HQ DOURLERS	22 Nov 1918 (contd)		A party under 2/Lt Rothery left for Dieppe to bring up the Battn's surplus stores left there. No 1. Company was lectured by 2nd Lt Howell on the subject of the coming Parliamentary Elections at 17.30 hours.	
	23rd Nov 1918		The area allotted to the Battalion having been cleared, no salvage work was done today. The Battalion carried out training including practice in "marching past." A notice was received from Division asking for the name of an Officer for attachment to the 250 Bde. R.F.A. for two weeks. The name of 2/Lieut. A.F. Gowers was submitted. A roll of candidates for instruction in workshops, which are to be erected at LANDRECIES, was asked for, the trades in question being carpenters and sawyers. Instructions with regard to the Educational Scheme were received. An Educational Officer to be appointed for the Battalion, and various returns with the object of finding Instructions in the Battalion, were asked for. Orders were received that defensive works could now be dismantled, and farmers given access to fields with permission to fill in trenches and remove entanglements. 2/Lieut. A.F. Gowers who had proceeded to the XIII Corps Infantry School, reported back, the course having been cancelled.	
	Sunday 24th Nov 1918		Voluntary Church services were held. 2/Lieut. Hunt was appointed to act as Educational Officer for the Battalion and an Education Bureau was established.	prot

Army Form C. 2118.

3RD ROYAL FUSILIERS

WAR DIARY
or
INTELLIGENCE SUMMARY.
(Erase heading not required.)

Place	Date	Hour	Summary of Events and Information	Remarks and references to Appendices
B.N. H.Q. DOURGES	24 Nov 1918 (contd)		2/Lieut. Ogden was appointed as Information Officer to deal with all questions connected with the forthcoming General Election. A notice of the "Active Service Army Schools" was received showing its aim. A supply of leaflets on various Educational subjects connected with the war was received.	
	25 Nov 1918		A conference of Commanding Officers and Battalion Educational Officers was held at Brigade, and subsequently the Commanding Officer held a conference with his Company Commanders and explained to them the system to be followed in the Educational Scheme. Instructions as to procedure for transferring men to Class W of Army Reserve for work in coal mines at home, were received. Company Commanders lectured their men on the subject of the forthcoming Elections and also explained to them the Educational Scheme with the object of assisting men to make up their minds as to their occupations after the war. A List of Honours and Awards was received; the following men of the Battalion have received the Military Medal:— 3956 Pte. M. Leggett 5931 Pte. C. Loden 13892 Cpl. E. Bryan 72611 Pte. A. Bones. 14758 " W. Evans. 4785 Pte. J. Lack. 8828 Pte. H. Gowers. 14631 " A. Mann. 13806 Cpl. E. Bishop. 63171 L/cpl. J. Cone. 13723 Sgt. W. Langley. 3763 Pte. F. Faulshaw 14190 Pte. P. Skeen. 12589 Pte. H. Balmer. mor	

Army Form C. 2118.

WAR DIARY
or
INTELLIGENCE SUMMARY.
(Erase heading not required.)

3RD ROYAL FUSILIERS

Instructions regarding War Diaries and Intelligence Summaries are contained in F.S. Regs., Part II. and the Staff Manual respectively. Title pages will be prepared in manuscript.

Place	Date	Hour	Summary of Events and Information	Remarks and references to Appendices
	25 Nov 1918 (continued)		2/Lieut. Bone reported back from leave in France. 2/Lieut. White of the 149 Brigade Light T.M.B. reported for duty on return from leave, the T.M.B. having been disbanded during his absence. The following officers were granted the right to wear the badges of the rank of Captain having been recommended for acting rank by the Divisional Commander:- T/Lieutenant R.B. Rudney. T/Lieutenant B.W. Tanner.	JML
	26 Nov 1918.		The Commanding Officer saw all men in the Battalion who had been Coal Miners and who were eligible for transfer to Army Reserve, Class "W", after medical examination six men with longest service were chosen to appear before examining officers tomorrow. A report on the progress of the Educational Scheme was sent in to Brigade. A Battalion Reading Room was instituted, and a supply of books having been obtained. A Battalion Library was started. A list of Honours and Rewards was received. The following Officers have been awarded the Military Cross:- Lieut. (a/Captain) A.M.H. Gordon. Lieut. (a/Captain) C.H. Braithache. Lieutenant A.S. Balding. Captain A.M.H. Gordon left on leave to England.	JML

Army Form C. 2118.

WAR DIARY
or
INTELLIGENCE SUMMARY.
(Erase heading not required.)

3RD ROYAL FUSILIERS

Instructions regarding War Diaries and Intelligence Summaries are contained in F. S. Regs., Part II. and the Staff Manual respectively. Title pages will be prepared in manuscript.

Place	Date	Hour	Summary of Events and Information	Remarks and references to Appendices
	26 Nov. 1918.		The following officers joined the Battalion on posting:- 2/Lieutenant C. J. Newton 2/Lieutenant C. A. Roberts. 2/Lieutenant J. Morrison.	m2
	27 Nov. 1918.		The Divisional Commander inspected the Battalion's Reading and Recreation Rooms, interior economy, billets and Transport, starting at 10.00 hours. In connection with the Educational Scheme classes were started in Book-keeping and Banking, and men also started to obtain instruction in the Regimental Workshops. The Commanding Officer held a conference of Company Commanders and explained further to them the proposed Educational Scheme as it affects the Battalion, and also explained to all Officers the need for their assistance as Instructors. The Divisional Commander expressed satisfaction with the arrangements in the Billets for feeding, recreation-rooms, billets, etc. He was very pleased with the condition of the Transport. The following letter was received from the Brigadier General:- The following is an extract from the 4th Army Commander, Gen. Sir H. Rawlinson to our Divisional Commander. "I would like to add what I had not an opportunity of saying the other evening, namely, how much I appreciate the splendid work that has been done by the 30th Division since they came into the battle at the end of September. The excellent services rendered by	m2

Army Form C. 2118.

WAR DIARY
or
INTELLIGENCE SUMMARY.
(Erase heading not required.)

3RD ROYAL FUSILIERS

Instructions regarding War Diaries and Intelligence Summaries are contained in F. S. Regs., Part II. and the Staff Manual respectively. Title pages will be prepared in manuscript.

Place	Date	Hour	Summary of Events and Information	Remarks and references to Appendices
	27 Nov 1918 (cont?)		The Division, from Prospect Hill at the beginning of October, to LE CATEAU and the MORMAL FOREST, has filled me with admiration and the gallantry of the Battalions and the determination and driving power of the Division as a whole is deserving of the highest praise." I very much regret that you are not marching to the frontier with the Fourth Army, but I hope still that in some future time you may join us again". "I am very glad that the good work done by your Battalion has met with such well deserved recognition".	AW2
	28 Nov 1918		Ten men who had been Coal Miners were accepted by the Examining Officers for transfer to Army Reserve Class W. A French class was started under the Educational Scheme, and other classes were continued as before.	AW2
	29 Nov.		The Battalion was paraded at 13.40 hours, and the Divisional Commander presented Medal Ribbons to the following Officers and men:- Captain C.A. Raithache. 3956 Pte. Leggett M. 14758 Pte Evans W. 14490 Pte Shean T. 13725 Sgt Langley W. 7/122 " Lack J. 14631 " Mann A. 13892 Cpl. Bryson J. 63171 L/C Eone J. 5931 " Lorder C. 72611 Pte Bones A. 4785 Pte Viner A. The following additional classes were started under the Educational Scheme :- Electricity and Telephony. Wireless.	AW2

WAR DIARY or INTELLIGENCE SUMMARY

3RD ROYAL FUSILIERS

Army Form C. 2118.

Place	Date	Hour	Summary of Events and Information	Remarks and references to Appendices
	Nov 29th 1918		Orders received that His Majesty the King would visit the Divisional Area on Sunday next. 2/Lieut. D.H. Sweetman reported from leave.	MD
	Nov 30th 1918		The Battalion paraded at 10.30 hours and lined up the positions which they will be in during the visit of His Majesty the King tomorrow. A miniature range having been constructed, Lewis shooting was started. Orders were received relaxing the Censorship Rules and allowing names of places to be mentioned. 2/Lieut. O.J.M'Kiernan reported back from hospital. The following officers joined on posting :— Lieut. A.S. Ewart. 2/Lieut. G.E. Dimond. 2/Lieut. H.D. Page. 2/Lieut. L.F. Cannon. 2/Lieut. W. Lewis. Total Casualties since Oct: 4th 1918. Killed, Officers 13 OR 53. Wounded, Officers 10 OR 302. Missing OR 114. Total Officers 23 OR 369. Evacuated sick with Malaria. 12. Evacuated sick with other causes. 33. Fighting Strength on November 30th 1918:— Officers 35. O. Ranks 522.	MD

Malcolm D.C.
Capt a/ Royal Fusiliers

3rd. Royal Fusiliers. SECRET.
Preliminary Instruction. No. 1.

Map reference
57A, N.W.

Appendix No. I

1. In the forthcoming operations
   No. 1 Company will be on the Right.
   No. 4 Company   "   "   "   Left.
   No. 3 Company   "   "   in Support.
   No. 2 Company   "   "   in Reserve.

2. No. 3 Company will continue to hold the line until Y/Z night, when O.C. No. 3 Company will arrange to withdraw all posts by 12 midnight, inside the barrage line (G9c.15.95), and to a previously reconnoitred line of posts on the forming up line G8B.25.00 to G8A.95.55.

3. A separate diagram is issued showing the formation and distances during the advance and the method of forming up at the jumping off ground.

4. As the forming up line is parallel to the line of the barrage and is not at right angles to the line of advance, Company Commanders will arrange to move their companies in echelon from the right.
   Direction must be taken by the compass and by prominent landmarks.
   Compass bearing (magnetic) to Road Junction ROSIMBOIS – LANDRECIES Road G10C.9.1 is 119 degrees.
   From G19C.9.1 to G11D.4.0 is 103 degrees.
   A separate diagram will be issued showing roads crossing the front of the Battalion during the advance and distance between each road. This diagram should be explained to every man and committed to memory.

5. Companies will move to their "jumping-off" ground in the order
   No. 4.
   No. 1.
   No. 2. This company will move up by small parties and will occupy cellars now occupied by Nos. 1 and 4 companies.
   Move to be completed by 3 p.m.
   O.C. No. 3. Company will arrange to reconnoitre the route to and position of the Forming up Ground.

6. Officers commanding Nos. 1 and 4 companies will arrange to have gaps cut in the hedges on their line of advance as far as is possible. White tape will be tied to the trees and hedges to show the Support and Reserve companies the line of advance. This should be done throughout the advance. Where tape is not available trees should be scarred:-
   Four cuts for No. 4 company.
   One broad cut for No. 1. company.

7. Arrangements are being made to bring up 70 picks and 120 shovels, and an extra supply of Lewis Gun drums, on Tanks.

Preliminary Instruction. No. 1. (contd).
----

8. When ammunition is urgently required by the leading companies, this should be passed up from the Supports and Reserves, who in turn will replace by ammunition taken from casualties.

9. All ranks must be warned that it is for the safety and welfare of the whole force that Verey Lights and Red flares should be shown at the different stages of the advance.

10. Three Tanks of "A" Company 9th Battalion Tank Corps will assist the Battalion.
Nos. will be I3 - I4 - I8.

11. One section 50th Battn. Machine Gun Corps will be attached to the Battalion, and will be employed in protecting and assisting the right flank of the Brigade.

12. Two forward guns of A and B Batteries 104 A.F.A. Brigade will assist the Battalion. Company Commanders will inform Headquarters when assistance is required and the nature of the target. Failing such information, the guns will be sent forward to select their own targets and assist the infantry as circumstances dictate.

13. Liaison Posts will be established at:-
G16A.95.65) to connect with
G17D.80.80) the 25th. Division.
The 1/8th. Royal Warwickshire Regiment will be on the right of the Battalion.
Both Support and Reserve Companies will pay especial attention to their right flank and keep Battalion Hdqrs informed as to the situation on that flank.

14. The leading platoons will fire White Verey Lights.
(1) On reaching the bend in the railway G9D.9.5.
(2) On reaching the road through G10C. and A.

2nd. November, 1918.

(signed) F. Parker. Captain.
A/Adjutant. S O M I.

3" Royal Fusiliers

3rd. Battalion Royal Fusiliers.

ORDER OF BATTLE - November 1st. 1918.

Headquarters:-

    Commanding   Lieut. Colonel. M.O.Clarke. D.S.O.
    Acting Adjutant   Lieutenant (A/Captain) F.Parker.
    Intelligence Officer 2/Lieutenant A.D.Calder.
    Medical Officer   Lieutenant M.Tylor. R.A.M.C.

No.1. Company:-

    Commanding   Captain R.M.Large.

No.2. Company:-

    Commanding   Lieutenant B.W.Tanner.

No.3. Company:-

    Commanding   Lieutenant R.E.Pudney.

No.4. Company:-

    Commanding   Lieutenant D.S.Corlett.

3rd Royal Fusiliers.   SECRET.

Preliminary Instruction – No. 2.

Appendix. 4.

1. The Battalion will take part in an operation which will be carried out on a front of about 50 miles.

2. Objectives and boundaries have been shewn on maps already issued to companies.

3. The attack will be carried out under a creeping barrage advancing at 100 yards in 6 minutes, to the RED LINE.
The barrage will open on the line G9C.1.6 to G2A.6.9, and will stand for 4 minutes on this line before advancing.

4. At Z plus 300 minutes the 151st Brigade will pass through the 150 – 149 Brigades and will capture the GREEN LINE.

5. The Scottish Horse will attack on the left of the Battalion, and the Royal Dublin Fusiliers will be in Reserve.

6. The 3rd. Royal Fusiliers will advance without pause to the RED LINE reaching it at Z plus 196 minutes. The barrage will then cease on that front.
On reaching this line the companies on the front line will push forward posts to assist the Royal Dublin Fusiliers in their task.
The Scottish Horse are pushing forward to the RED LINE at Zero plus 214 minutes.
The barrage will cease when the RED LINE is reached.

7. The 2nd Royal Dublin Fusiliers remain in Reserve until the 3rd Royal Fusiliers have gained their objective.
On the capture of the RED LINE, positions will be consolidated in depth and will continue until the 151st Inf. Brigade are established on the GREEN LINE. The 149th. Brigade will then concentrate about HAUTE CORNEE.

8. At Zero plus 205 fire will cease on the Red Dotted Line for 5 minutes. Intense fire will open at Z plus 210 minutes for a period of 4 minutes. This will indicate the hour for the next advance.

9. Tanks operating with the 3rd Royal Fusiliers will be in position on the Infantry Jumping-off Line by Zero. Their objective will be the line of trees in G11B and G12A and D – thence working southwards to Canal Bank to establish posts in H7C.

10. Two Stokes Mortar Guns and 200 rounds of ammunition will be available on whichever flank they may be required.

11. Contact planes will call for flares:-
    (1) At Z plus 2 hours on RED DOTTED LINE.
    (2) At Z plus 5 hours on RED LINE.
    (3) At Z plus 6 hours to verify above.
    (4) At 1400 and 1600 hours between RED and GREEN LINES.

12. The Main Line of Communication will be from FONTAINE – Drill Ground Corner Route de LANDRECIES.

13.a. In the event of a counter attack, counter attack patrol aeroplanes will drop white parachute lights over the centre of the hostile troops.

13.b. Contact planes will call for flares:-
    At Z plus 2 hours   on Red Dotted Line.
    At Z plus 5 hours   on Red Line.
    At Z plus 6 hours   to verify above.
    Flares must be lit clear of the trees and scrub. When troops run short of flares they must wave their tin helmets.

3rd Royal Fusiliers - Preliminary Instruction No. 2. (contd).

14. <u>Headquarters.</u> Battalion Headquarters will move along the line of the inter-Battalion boundary, and will be established with the Scottish Horse at G9A.45.15 after the line Drill Ground - LANDRECIES Road has been reached. Thence positions will be taken up at G9D.50.90 and G10C.80.60, according as the advance continues.

3rd. Royal Fusiliers.   SECRET.

Operation Order No. 4.

Appendix. 6.

1. Zero will be at 06.15 hours.

2. As the 25th Division is at 05.45 hours calculations will be made from this hour to avoid the German barrage.

3. Companies will be in position on the Forming-up ground by Zero minus 60 minutes.

4. The order of movement to the tape will be :- No. 4 - No. 1 - No. 2. No. 3. Coy will be in position on the Line and will be in support to the leading companies.

5. No. 3. Coy will withdraw all posts so as to be inside the barrage line by 05.30 hours.

6. Company Commanders will ensure that no movement takes place in the forming-up area after 05.30. A report will be sent by runner to Battn. Hdqrs when each company is in position. Each company should allow half an hour to get into their battle positions.

7. Support and Reserve Companies will pay particular care to the mopping up of all ground in rear of the leading companies, and a careful lookout should be kept for snipers in trees.

8. The Reserve Company (No. 2 .) will NOT advance beyond the road in G9A and C until the leading companies have cleared the high ground and ridge in G9D. This ridge will be held by No. 2 company until our line has reached the line of the Drill Ground - LANDRECIES Road.

9. On reaching the RED LINE one section of machine guns, No. 5 Section "B" Company Machine Gun Corps under 2/Lieut. Holt, will come into action and assist in consolidation.

3rd November, 1918.

(signed) F. Parker.   Captain.
Acting Adjutant, SOMI.

O.C. No. 2. Coy.
SOMI.

Appendix No. 7.

November 4th, 1918.
12.25 hours.

1. Your message timed 11.30 just received.

2. The Germans are reported on the run and the 25th. Division have crossed the Canal.

3. The Brigade have ordered us to occupy the Belt of Trees in G 11 B and G 12 Central, and to occupy the Spur in G 12 D.

4. Your company and all the Dublin Fusiliers available are to push on and carry out this operation as soon as possible. This line will become the final objective of the Dublin Fusiliers supported by ourselves.

5. It will NOT be necessary to employ the whole of your force for this purpose.

6. The Scottish Horse will be responsible for clearing the belt of trees from G11B.3.7 to the track in G12A.3.5.
The Royal Fusiliers to G12Central, and you will be prepared to support the Scottish Horse.
The Dublin Fusiliers will clear the spur from G12Central to G12D.9.5.

7. These orders assume that your casualties have not been very severe, and that you are capable of exploiting a very great success. Show these orders to the Dublin Fusiliers and Scottish Horse whose Colonel is aware of the orders given.

3rd. Battalion Royal Fusiliers.
Battalion Orders.   Appendix. 8.

1. The 149th. Brigade has established a line from the Spur in G12D along the line of the trees in G12A and G11B.

2. A section of Machine Guns is established in H7C33 to command the bridgeheads at H7B2.2 and H13 A.55.

2. Two machine guns are in position protecting the 3 flanks of the Battalion. 3 sections in addition will be available to cover our front.

3. It is of the utmost importance to seize the bridgeheads mentioned in para 2. The Royal Dublin Fus-iliers have been ordered to carry out this task forthwith.

4. No. 2 Company will be ready to assist the Royal Dublin Fusiliers if required in establishing the Bridgehead in H7B.2.2 . Should this bridgehead NOT have been seized on receipt of these orders, No. 2 Company will send out a platoon to seize it and make good the crossing.

5. No. 2. company will hold its present front line as an outpost line. No. 3. company will move up in close support and occupy a line of posts on the high ground immediately North of the track in G12C central.

6. Nos 1 and 4 companies will be formed into one company under the command of 2/Lieut. SAVOURS. This composite company will be called No.1. Company and will remain on its present line and will be in Reserve.

7. One Army Brigade R.F.A is covering the front with an S.O. S. Line about 200 yards East of the bridgeheads.

8. The Reserve Company will furnish a carrying party of 25 men to report to Battn. Hdqrs at 7 7.30 p.m. to carry up rations and ammunition.

9. Companies will report exact location of company headquarters.

10. Nos. 2 and 3 companies will send out patrols and ascertain the general line of enemy positions, using the railway for direction, and arranging with the Royal Dublin Fusiliers for patrolling the East side of the railway, and the Scottish Horse on the West side of the Laie de la Pepiniere.

11. No orders have yet been received regarding further movements but companies must be prepared to move on and exploit our success at short notice.

12. Empty Lewis Gun Drums must be returned to Battn. Hdqr s at once for refilling.

13. Usual situation reports will be rendered at 3 a.m.

            Issued at 19.05 hours to all
            companies and 149 Inf. Bde.   Nov. 4th, 1918.

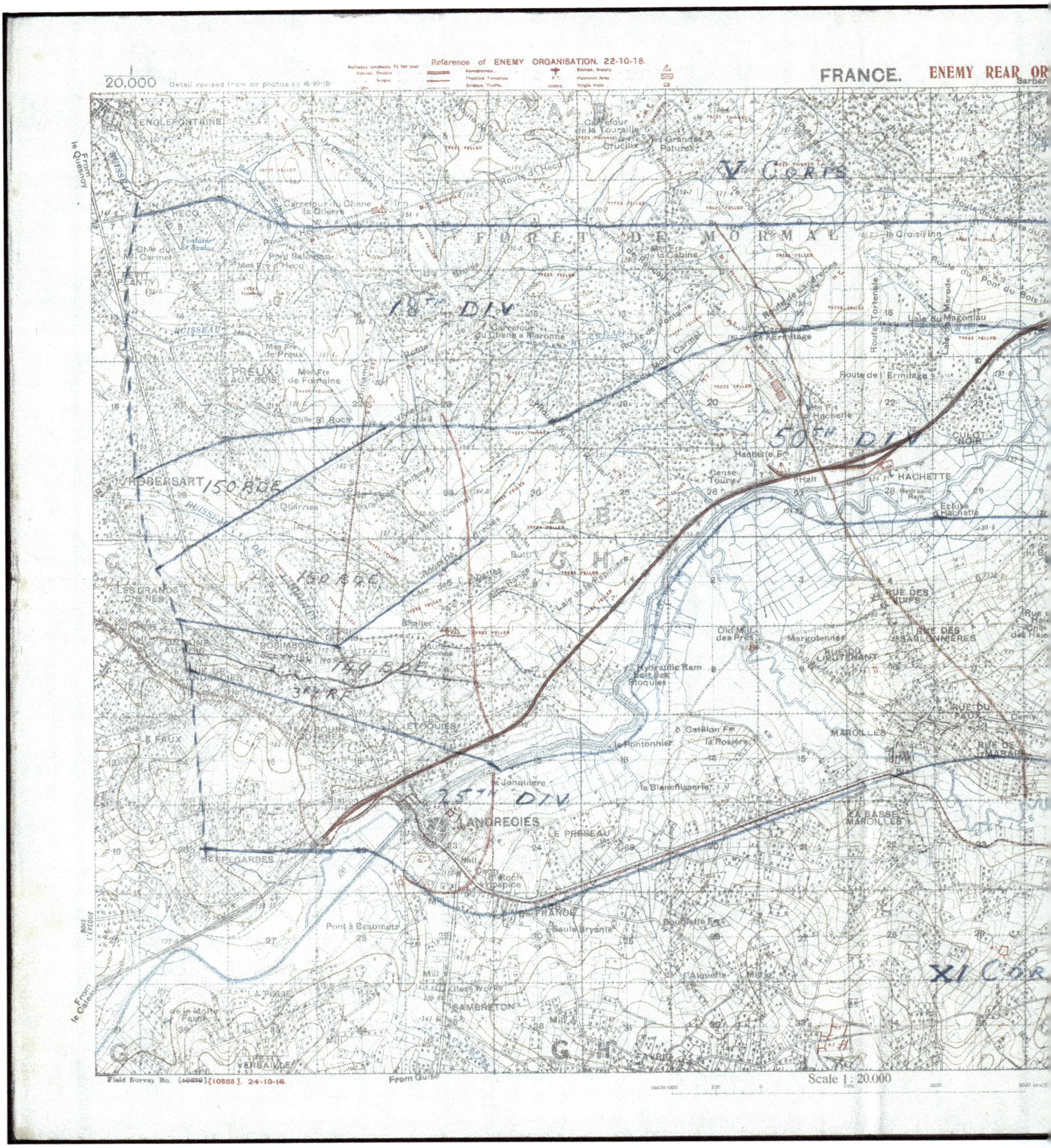

FRANCE.
ENEMY REAR OR
Reference of ENEMY ORGANISATION. 22-10-18.
1/20,000
Detail revised from air photos to 16-10-18.
ENGLEFONTAINE
FORET DE MORMAL
V CORPS
18TH DIV
150 BDE
149 BDE
50TH DIV
25TH DIV
XI COR
PREUX AUX BOIS
ROBERSART
LANDRECIES
HACHETTE
MAROILLES
SAMBRETON
FONTAINE
Field Survey Bn. [10885]. 24-10-18.
Scale 1 : 20,000
From Guise
From le Quesnoy
From le Cateau

3rd. Royal Fusiliers. SECRET.
Order - No. 5.
                                          Appendix. 1.

1. At 06.30 the 5th inst., the 151st Brigade now on the GREEN LINE will continue its advance in conjunction with the 18th Division, and will complete the capture of that portion of the Divisional objective N of the SAMBRE, bounded on the North by LAIE du MAGONIAU and on South and East by River SAMBRE, pushing out a post to Lock in B18D. A bridgehead will be established at ECLUSE DE HACHETTE in B28D.
The 25th Division on the right will push out to the spur in H14-H15-H21.

2. The 149th Brigade is moving off to about CENSE TOURY B26B, prepared to cross the River in the vicinity of HACHETTE FARM.

3. Starting point G6D.0.1.
Order of march of Brigade:-
Scottish Horse   0700 hours 5th.
3/Royal Fusiliers   0705 "   "
2/R.Dublin Fusiliers
less one company   0710 "   "
149 Trench Mortar Battery 0 713 hours 5th.
Route:- Rifle range, and continuation to cross roads in B20C - CENSE TOURY.

4. Companies will collect under company arrangements, under cover from view by 0600 hours, and will move off independently in the following order:-
No. 2 Company by line of belt of trees and across country direct to SAW MILLS.
No. 3 Company   - ditto-
No. 1 Company - across country direct to SAW MILLS.
Companies will be formed up in close column of companies immediately South of railway track G11A 90.85 by 0650 hours.

5. Officers chargers A and B groups 1st. Line Transport will be at SAW MILLS at 0650 hours under orders issued by Brigade Transport Officer.

6. Officers should carry map sheet 57A 1/40,000.

7. Companies will send parties to Battn. Hdqrs at 0600 hours to draw any ammunition which they require to complete. This can then be distributed at the starting point.

8. Companies will report to Battn. Hdqrs when they move off.

9. Acknowledge.

    Issued at 0230 hours Nov, 5th.

Appendix. 1.

3rd. Royal Fusiliers.
Order No. 6.

1. The Division is advancing to the Brown Line, i.e. CHAUSSEE BRUNHAUT C6C12-D13, Sheet 57.A 1/40,0 00.
A company of Scottish Horse consisting of 3 Officers and 100 O.R cross the SAMBRE at B27Central and move to C13D08 along the towpath. They leave this point at 07.15 hours at which time the 150th Brigade will cross the HELPE River in vicinity of Hte NOYELLES. The Scottish Horse (1 company) advance to the spur in C16C and obtain touch Southwards with 150 Brigade.

2. 3rd Royal Fusiliers and Scottish Horse (less 1 company) will cross CANAL BRIDGE B27D.05.80 in that order, head of column crossing at 07.00 hours, and proceed via Road Junction B11C.1.6 - Rue des HAIES - Hte NOYELLES to position gained by company of Scottish Horse.

3. Thence the 3rd Royal Fusiliers (on the right) and Scottish Horse (on the left) will attack and capture LEVAL, after capturing which the advance will be continued due Eastwards to the BROWN LINE. Right of 3rd Royal Fusiliers on road at D19B.5.5, 2/Royal Dublin Fusiliers will be in Brigade Reserve.

4. One section of "A" Battery 104 Brigade A.F.A will be attached to the Battalion, also one section of M.Gs.

5. The Battalion will parade at 0645 hours in the following order:-
No. 2., No. 1., No. 3. one section of M.Gs., one section of 18 pdrs.

6. No. 2. Company will be prepared to act as Advanced Guard to the Column.

7. The attack on LEVAL will be made on a one company front
No. 2. Company attacking
No. 1. Company in Support.
No. 3. Company in Reserve.

8. In the advance Eastward to the BROWN LINE No. 2. Coy will be on the Right, No. 1. Coy on the Left, and No. 3. Coy prepared to support on either flank.

9. Three Lewis Gun Limbers will accompany the Battalion - Companies will carry tools in the proportion laid down.

10. No. 3. Coy will detail an Officer with 4 runners to keep touch with the attacking troops of the 150 Brigade on our right flank. He will keep Battn. Hdqrs informed of the progress of operations.

Issued at 05.00 hours. November 6th.

Appendix. 1.

Message of congratulation received from the Army Commander and Divisional Commander, November 7th, 1918.

The following message from Army Commander dated Nov. 5th will be communicated to all ranks:-
"Please convey to 50th. Division my congratulations on their success today in forcing their way through the Forest of Mormal; the gallantry and determination of the troops is deserving of high praise".

The Divisional Commander wishes to thank all ranks for what they did yesterday.

Orders issued to O.C. No. 2. Company, Nov. 6th, 1918.

Appendix. 2.

1. Runner reports you are in position on right of Scottish Horse.

2. You are to push through LEVAL and get into touch with 33rd Division. They don't intend to <u>hold</u> it according to a prisoner just captured.

3. Your right will be in touch with Scottish Horse, and you may employ No. 1. Company to operate on your left. When you are in touch with 33rd Division, you will advance on railway and BROWN LINE.

4. Your right boundary with Scottish Horse will be East and West on a line drawn through points 250 yards North of C16-17-18 Central.

5. The 33rd Division have captured PETIT MAUBEUGE. Two guns are now in position to support you.

6. Let me know position in LEVAL.

7. Boundary between No. 2 and No.1. companies East of LEVAL will be Road junction C10C.5.4 along road by river to where river is crossed by railway; thence due East along ground line C11C5.0 to BROWN LINE.

12.00 hours.

Appendix 3.

Message to 149th. Infy. Brigade from 3rd Royal Fusiliers.

R.F.8. November 6th.   Map Ref. 57 A. 1/40,000 AAA Two companies dug in in section posts 200 yards east of the BROWN LINE from C12D70.85 to junction with 3 3rd Division AAA Right company held up by M.G. fire consolidated along road from G12D to C12D0.7 AAA Have ordered company to take up position on BROWN LINE from Cross Roads C12D7.9 to left flank of Scottish Horse D13A4.6 AAA If 33rd Div could take over left company front it would help AAA Two prisoners captured while going round line.

1850 p.m.

Appendix. 1.

To BUZE   R.F. 63.   8.   AAA

Situation as follows AAA 3 companies in line along line of sunken road in E.14.C and E.20.A with 2 M.Gs on either flank AAA Platoon on North side of Mt. DOURLERS has NOT yet been found AAA Patrols sent up to gain touch with QIGE and liaison post ordered out to L of Mt. DOURLERS to connect with QIGE AAA Left company has been ordered to advance to line of road running from L of DOURLERS to E.14.D.0.0 As I now have no reserve will try and push out to high ground and make sunken road reserve line each company dropping a platoon but companies are too weak to hold front of 1200 yards with only 220 men AAA

       SOMI   20.10.

Appendix. 2.

To   O.C. No. 2. Company.

    R.F. 69   9   AAA

HUITHIAU has been occupied by Scottish Horse AAA Push forward by bounds moving by roads or tracks AAA Secure ground on Western edge of FOREST of BEUGNIES and push through Forest to gain objective at dawn unless you can do so without opposition parties AAA Report progress frequently AAA Battalion Headquarters will move via MONT DOURLERS through E.15.C to farm E.21.B.9.0 at HUITHIAU AAA Artillery have been ordered to cease fire and m.gs. take up position on Hill 202. AAA

            SOMI.   02.00.

Appendix. 3.

Message from 3rd Royal Fusi-liers to 149 Inf. Brigade.

To BUZE

R.F. 68   9   AAA

Royal Fusiliers are now on line L of DOURLERS - line of posts E of road in E24D58 to E14D00 thence down to fork road in E20C AAA I have ordered all 3 companies to at once push out patrols along roads and make ground by definite bounds from point to point AAA To make good "line of resistance" before dawn and then push through FOREST of BEUGNIES AAA No artillery fire on West edge of Forest of BEUGNIES after 3 a.m.   AAA

SOMI.   0215.

(6392) Wt. W6192/P875 1,500,000 4/18 McA & W Ltd (E 2815) Forms W3091/4. Army Form W.3091.

48.C.
(13 sheets)

Vol 7

Cover for Documents.

Nature of Enclosures.

War Diary

3RD BATTALION ROYAL FUSILIERS.

DECEMBER. - 1918.

Appendices. - Nil.

Notes, or Letters written.

Army Form C. 2118.

WAR DIARY

INTELLIGENCE SUMMARY

(Erase heading not required.)

3RD BATTALION ROYAL FUSILIERS

Instructions regarding War Diaries and Intelligence Summaries are contained in F. S. Regs. Part II. and the Staff Manual respectively. Title pages will be prepared in manuscript.

Place	Date	Hour	Summary of Events and Information	Remarks and references to Appendices
DOURLERS	Dec.1, 1918		The Battalion paraded at 10.55 hours and marched to a field South and East of the SEMOUSIES, DOURLERS – MAUBEUGE, AVESNES Cross Roads E.19.B.7.7, where they together with other Units of the 149th Inf. Brigade Group, were visited by His Majesty the King. The King arrived about 11.45 hours and was accompanied by the Prince of Wales, Prince Albert, and their staff. The Commanding Officer had the honour of being presented to His Majesty, who also spoke to several N.C.Os and men of the Battalion. After staying about 20 minutes The King left in his car amidst very hearty cheering. A voluntary Church Service was held in the evening.	
"	Dec.2, 1918		10 Officers and 200 Other Ranks of the Battalion attended a Lecture by Dr. Irvine on the Problems involved on Demobilization and Reconstruction at 11.30 hours. Official notification was received that 2/Lieut. F.N. ROBERTS had died of wounds in hospital in Liverpool.	

Army Form C. 2118.

WAR DIARY
or
~~INTELLIGENCE SUMMARY~~

3RD BATTALION ROYAL FUSILIERS

(Erase heading not required.)

Place	Date	Hour	Summary of Events and Information	Remarks and references to Appendices
DOURLERS	Dec.2 (cont'd)		Major W.A. TRASENSTER left for PARIS on leave. 2/Lieut. J.T. MORRIS reported back from duty as Area Commandant of BAS LIEU.	
	Dec. 3		A Sports Conference was held at Brigade Headquarters in the morning - Captain E.A.W. HUGHES represented the Battalion.

An additional class - on Gardening - was started under the Educational Scheme.

The Battalion Concert Party gave their first performance in a Hall near Brigade Headquarters, at 17.30 hours.

Notification was received that the Brigade would move to DOMPIERRE on the 5th.inst, and would take over Billets from the 4th. K.R.R. Corps.

A Lecture was given by the Quartermaster to all Subaltern Officers on the subject of Rations, at 16.00 hours. | (m)? |

Army Form C. 2118.

WAR DIARY
or
INTELLIGENCE SUMMARY.
(Erase heading not required.)

3rd BATTALION ROYAL FUSILIERS.

Instructions regarding War Diaries and Intelligence Summaries are contained in F. S. Regs., Part II. and the Staff Manual respectively. Title pages will be prepared in manuscript.

Place	Date	Hour	Summary of Events and Information	Remarks and references to Appendices
DOURLERS	Dec. 4		A Billeting party proceeded to DOMPIERRE in the morning to reconnoitre billets for the Battalion tomorrow. Detailed orders were received as to the move. A List of Honours and Awards was received; the following were awarded the Military Medal:- 23688 L/Corporal R. Harris. 9685 A/L.C.G. Porter. 15050 Private G. Doe. 96348 Private J. Harsent. Capt. HUGHES lectured the Battalion on "The meaning of Empire", at 11.30 hours. The following letter was received by the Commanding Officer from Major-General Sir. G. BARTON, K.C.V.O., C.B., C.M.G., Colonel of the Regiment:- "I wish to congratulate all ranks of the Third Battalion on their splendid record of Service, both on the Western Front and in SALONICA, as well as on their many brilliant engagements which have added glory to the History of the Regiment."	[M2]
Battln. Hqrs. DOMPIERRE. Map. 57A J.7.A.B	Dec. 5		The Battalion moved starting at 09.20 hours, to new Billets in DOMPIERRE (six Kilometres N.W. of AVESNES). No. 3 Company was subsequently moved to LE PETIT FUCHAU, in order to provide more accommodation in the DOMPIERRE area. Owing to the fact that the 50th Machine Gun Company as well as the 3rd Royal Fusiliers had to find billets in the same area as was vacated by the K.R.R. Corps.	[M2]

Army Form C. 2118.

WAR DIARY
or
INTELLIGENCE SUMMARY.

3RD BATTALION ROYAL FUSILIERS

Place	Date	Hour	Summary of Events and Information	Remarks and references to Appendices
DOMPIERRE.	Dec 5. (cont'd)		Great difficulty was found in providing accommodation.	
"	Dec. 6.		A Recreation Room was established in the new area, and arrangements were made to continue the Educational Classes. 2/Lieut. H.W. Howell returned from leave at Paris Plage, and another vacancy for this leave was notified to us.	MD
"	Dec. 7.		The Commanding Officer attended a conference of Commanding Officers at Brigade Headquarters at 14.00 hours. Companies carried out training according to the Programme of Work, and Educational Classes were restarted. Arrangements were made for sending home tomorrow the four following N.C.Os:- 11956 Sgt. Weedon. F. 5384 Sgt. Pepper. F. 14909 Cpl. Eagle. B. 14875 Cpl. Chapman. E. under the scheme for exchange of "War-worn" N.C.Os.	MD
"	Dec. 8.		Two men proceeded to XIII Corps Workshops at LANDRECIES on Carpentry courses under the Educational Scheme.	MD

Army Form C. 2118.

WAR DIARY
or
INTELLIGENCE SUMMARY.
(Erase heading not required.)

3rd BATTALION ROYAL FUSILIERS

Place	Date	Hour	Summary of Events and Information	Remarks and references to Appendices
DOMPIERRE	Dec. 8		Demobilization papers were received in the case of 2/Lieut. G.E. White, who is to be held ready to proceed to a dispersal centre at home pending further instructions from the War Office.	
"	Dec. 9		A Voluntary Church Service was held in the evening. A further supply of books was received from the Divisional Lending Library in exchange for those at present in charge. A Riding Class for Officers was started - two Officers per company commenced to take instruction. Horses were lent by the O.C. 50th Machine Gun Corps. 2/Lieut. A.J. Gowers reported back from attachment to the 250th Brigade R.F.A. Captain A.E.W. Hughes (acting Adjutant) and 2/Lieut. G.E. White proceeded to hospital. The duties of acting Adjutant were taken over by 2/Lieut. J. Ogden during Captain Hughes' absence.	MD
"	Dec. 10		Brig. General Robinson visited the Battalion. He inspected the Educational Classes and certain of the men's billets. Nos 3 and 4 Companies went on a Route March of about six miles. Nos 1 and 2 Companies were engaged in company training	MD

Army Form C. 2118.

WAR DIARY
or
INTELLIGENCE SUMMARY.   3RD BATTALION ROYAL FUSILIERS
(Erase heading not required.)

Place	Date	Hour	Summary of Events and Information	Remarks and references to Appendices
DAMPIERRE	Dec. 11		In connection with the Parliamentary Election 576 Ballot papers have been received to date, of which number 158 have been actually delivered to men - the remainder being for men no longer with the Battalion. Nos. 1 and 2 Companies went on a 6 miles Route March. Nos. 3 and 4 Companies carried on company training according to Programme. Major W.A. Kassler M.C. returned from leave to Paris.	Mr
"	Dec. 12		The Commanding Officer attended a conference at Brigade Headquarters at 10.00 hours. Companies carried out training under company arrangements. 2/Lieut R.F. Letherby proceeded to the 50th Divisional Reception Camp to take up duties as Assistant Adjutant.	Mr
	Dec. 13		The Divisional Commander - Major General Jackson. D.S.O - accompanied by Brigadier General Robinson, visited the Battalion and inspected the men's Billets, Dining Rooms &c. The Commanding Officer lectured Nos 1 and 2 Companies on "Discipline".	Mr

WAR DIARY
or
INTELLIGENCE SUMMARY.

(Erase heading not required.)

Army Form C. 2118.

3RD BATTALION ROYAL FUSILIERS

Place	Date	Hour	Summary of Events and Information	Remarks and references to Appendices
DOMPIERRE	Dec. 14		Warning order received that 149th Brigade are to move to the LE QUESNOY area on the 18th inst.	MR
	Dec. 15		Companies engaged on Company Training and Kit inspections. The following Officers reported for duty:- 2/Lieut. M.S. Francis 2/Lieut. J.W. Myers	MR
			Voluntary Church services were held in the morning and evening. Lieut. Colonel M.O. Clarke. D.S.O. proceeded on leave to PARIS PLAGE.	
	Dec. 16		The Battalion paraded for a Battalion Route March. Lieut. S.A. Turner and 2nd Lieut. H.J. Stevens M.C. reported from leave. The Commanding Officer saw Company Commanders and Transport Officer and explained details of proposed move.	MR
	Dec. 17		Billeting party under Captain F.S. Lindsey left for LE QUESNOY at 0900 hours. Brigade Orders for move to LE QUESNOY on the 18th inst. were received. Advance Party left for LE QUESNOY at 0900 hours. Companies engaged in cleaning up billets and preparing for move.	MR

Army Form C. 2118.

WAR DIARY
or
INTELLIGENCE SUMMARY.   3RD BATTALION ROYAL FUSILIERS
(Erase heading not required.)

Place	Date	Hour	Summary of Events and Information	Remarks and references to Appendices
	Dec 18		Battalion moved to LE QUESNOY, starting at 07/15 hours and arriving there at 14.00 hours.	nil
LE QUESNOY			Lieut. S. A. Turner was appointed "Demobilization Officer" to deal with all matters touching Demobilization.	nil
	Dec 19		Companies engaged in cleaning up their own billets and the Billeting Area generally, everything being in a very filthy condition.	nil
	Dec 20		Companies again engaged in cleaning up and improving their billets. Education classes restarted. 2.d Lieut. Harlin appointed as Sanitation Officer in charge of all arrangements for cleaning our Area. An Officers Mess Meeting was held to settle questions in regard to a Battalion Officers Mess to be started in a few days.	nil
	Dec 21		Companies on various fatigues in connection with cleaning area. Work was continued all day in order to get things in order for Christmas.	nil
	Dec 22		A Parade Church Service was held in the morning, and Voluntary service in the evening. No sanitary work was done today.	nil

Army Form C. 2118.

WAR DIARY
or
INTELLIGENCE SUMMARY.   3RD BATTALION ROYAL FUSILIERS

(Erase heading not required.)

Instructions regarding War Diaries and Intelligence Summaries are contained in F. S. Regs., Part II. and the Staff Manual respectively. Title pages will be prepared in manuscript.

Place	Date	Hour	Summary of Events and Information	Remarks and references to Appendices
LE QUESNOY	Dec. 23		Sanitary work was continued by all companies. Nos 1 and 2. and Headquarters Company moved into the Barracks, and their previous Billet was taken over for Recreation Rooms &c.	MR
	Dec. 24		A Divisional Parade was held in the Square of the Barracks occupied by the Scottish Horse, and medal ribbons were presented by Major General Jackson to the following recipients:- Capt. A. McR. Gordon. M.C. 7156 C.S.M. A. Hannington. D.C.M. Capt. B.W. Tanner. M.C. 90372 Cpl. R. Shaw D.C.M. 2/Lieut. H.J. Savenna. M.C. 23688 Cpl. R. Harris. M.M. 2/Lieut. H.F. Letherby. M.C. 9685 L/Cpl. G. Porter. M.M. 15050 Pte. C. Boe. M.M. Lieut. Colonel M.O. Clarke, D.S.O. returned from leave at PARIS PLAGE.	MR
	Dec. 25.		A Brigade Church Parade was held at 1100 hours, and there were voluntary early morning and evening services. Brigadier General Robinson accompanied by the Commanding Officer visited the men's Christmas dinners at 13.00 hours.	MR
	Dec. 26.		This day was observed as a holiday for all ranks. 2/Lieut. Myers proceeded to hospital.	MR

Army Form C. 2118.

WAR DIARY
or
INTELLIGENCE SUMMARY

3RD BATTALION ROYAL FUSILIERS

(Erase heading not required.)

Place	Date	Hour	Summary of Events and Information	Remarks and references to Appendices
LE QUESNOY	Dec. 27		The Commanding Officer inspected the Billets of Nos. 3 and 4 Companies, and all the Officers Billets of those companies. Orders to commence Salvage work in the LE QUESNOY area were received. Lieut. S.A. Turner took over the duties of Acting Adjutant from 2/Lieut. J. Ogden and 2/Lieut. R. Stanaway the duties of Assistant Adjutant and Demobilization Officer vice Lieut. S.A. Turner.	M1
	Dec. 28		Companies engaged in cleaning and improving their billets and areas. The Commanding Officer interviewed Officers regarding their confidential reports.	M2
	Dec. 29		A Parade Service was held in the morning and Voluntary services in the evening. 2/Lieut. J.C. White rejoined the Battalion from hospital. 2/Lieut. J. Ogden left the Battalion to report to War Office to take up duty as Station Accountant in the Western Command. Following areas were allotted to Companies for Salvage, commencing tomorrow under "Brigade Salvage Scheme":— Ref Map 51; M.1.b; M.2.a and b; M.1.d; M.2.c and d; M.7.b; M.8.a and b; M.7.d; M.8.c and d.	M3

Army Form C. 2118.

WAR DIARY
or
INTELLIGENCE SUMMARY.
(Erase heading not required.)

3RD BATTALION ROYAL FUSILIERS

Place	Date	Hour	Summary of Events and Information	Remarks and references to Appendices
LE QUESNOY	Dec 29 (cont)		The Commanding Officer attended a conference at Brigade Headquarters. Confidential reports on Officers were forwarded to Brigade.	
	Dec. 30		Nos. 1 and 2 Coys salvaged the areas allotted to them. Nos. 3 and 4 Coys were at the disposal of Company Commanders for cleaning and improving billets. The Commanding Officer attended a Conference at Brigade Headquarters. Lieutenant & Qr. Mr. J. Best returned from leave to United Kingdom.	mm mm
	Dec. 31		No. 1 and No. 3 Companies salvaged the areas allotted to them. No. 2 and No. 4 Companies cleaned up billets and carried out 4 hours drill and training.	
			Fighting strength on Dec 31st 1918. Officers :- 30 Other Ranks :- 534	
				Admitted to hospital during month with Malaria :- 7 O.R. Admitted to hospital with other causes :- 50 O.R. mm

Mohanlal d/Lt Cmdt 3/ Royal Fusiliers

(6392) Wt. W6192/P875 1,500,000 4/18 McA & W Ltd (E 2815) Forms W3091/4.   Army Form W.3091.

49.C.
(9 sheets)

Cover for Documents.

Nature of Enclosures.

War Diary.

3rd Royal Fusiliers.

Appendices, Nil.

January - 1919.

Notes, or Letters written.

Army Form C. 2118.

WAR DIARY
~~INTELLIGENCE~~ SUMMARY.
(Erase heading not required.)

3RD ROYAL FUSILIERS

Instructions regarding War Diaries and Intelligence Summaries are contained in F. S. Regs., Part II. and the Staff Manual respectively. Title pages will be prepared in manuscript.

Place	Date	Hour	Summary of Events and Information	Remarks and references to Appendices
LE QUESNOY	Jan 1. 1919		Today was observed as a holiday for all ranks. The Divisional Commander, Major General Jackson, entertained 600 local school children in Nos 3 and 4 Companies Barracks. He expressed his gratification and appreciation of the manner in which the rooms had been decorated. AOS	
	Jan 2.		Nos 1 and 2 companies salvaged the areas allotted to them. Nos 3 and 4 companies were employed on various fatigue parties, the Battalions being on duty. The O.C. held a conference of all Company Commanders, and explained Demobilization Position and Cadre establishments. 2/Lieut W. H. Howell to duty with his company, the post of Assistant Educational Officer, being no longer necessary. 2/Lieut D.H. Sweetman admitted to hospital. AOS	
	Jan 3.		Nos 2 and 3 companies salvaged the areas allotted to them. Nos 1 and 4 companies were engaged on various fatigues and working parties. The Commanding Officer took over command of the 149th Brigade during the absence of the Brigadier on leave to U.K., Major Fraser, M.C. taking over command of the Battalion. AOS	

(A.cz66) W.tW5306/P773 750,000 2/15 Sch. 52 Forms/Can8/16
D. D. & L., London, E.C.

Army Form C. 2118.

WAR DIARY
or
INTELLIGENCE SUMMARY.
(Erase heading not required.)

3RD ROYAL FUSILIERS

Place	Date	Hour	Summary of Events and Information	Remarks and references to Appendices
LE QUESNOY	Jan. 4		Nos. 2 and 3 companies salvaged the areas allotted to them. Nos. 1 and 4 companies engaged in guards and fatigues and provided guards. The Battalion was on duty for the Brigade. Lieutenant J. Hart joined Battalion on posting. ws	
	Jan. 5		The Battalion paraded for Divine Service at 10.45 hours. ws	
	Jan. 6		Nos. 3 and 4 companies salvaged the areas allotted to them. No. 1 company held a Mobilization Inspection, No. 2 company being engaged with guards and fatigues. 2/Lieut. C.W. Bowell succeeded on leave to U.K. ws	
	Jan. 7		Nos. 1 and 4 companies salvaged the areas allotted to them. Nos. 2 and 3 companies were engaged in guards and fatigues. The Regimental Band and Bandmaster joined the Battalion from England. The Battalion was on duty for the Brigade. ws	
	Jan. 8		Nos. 1 and 2 companies salvaged the areas allotted to them. Nos. 3 and 4 companies were engaged in Guards and Fatigues. Lieut. G. P. Hunan 2/Lieut. N.G. Gowers D.C.M. and Colour Secnt joined the Battalion with the Regimental Colors from England. ws	

Army Form C. 2118.

WAR DIARY
or
INTELLIGENCE SUMMARY

3RD ROYAL FUSILIERS

(Erase heading not required.)

Instructions regarding War Diaries and Intelligence Summaries are contained in F.S. Regs., Part II. and the Staff Manual respectively. Title pages will be prepared in manuscript.

Place	Date	Hour	Summary of Events and Information	Remarks and references to Appendices
LE QUESNOY	Jan 8 (cont.) Jan 9		Nos. 2 and 3 companies salvaged the areas allotted to them. Nos. 1 and 4 companies were engaged on guards and fatigues.	
	Jan 10		Nos. 3 and 4 companies salvaged the areas allotted to them. Nos. 1 and 2 companies were engaged in guards and fatigues. The Battalion was on duty for the Brigade.	
	Jan 11		The Battalion paraded as strong as possible for rehearsal of Ceremony of Receiving the colours. 2/Lieut. R.L. le Maistre left the Battalion on A.V.L.T. for courses at 3rd Army Rifle School.	108.
	Jan 12		Battalion paraded for Church Parade in the morning. No salvaging was done.	
	Jan 13		Battalion paraded as strong as possible for the Ceremony of Receiving the colours. They were handed over by Lieut. Col. L. P. Evans and 2/Lieut. H.A. Garcia B.C.M. to 2/Lieut. Page and a Colour attendant. Capt. C.A. Barthacke M.C. left the Battalion for United Kingdom for demobilization. The Battalion was on duty for the Brigade.	109.

Army Form C. 2118.

WAR DIARY
or
INTELLIGENCE SUMMARY.
(Erase heading not required.)

2ND ROYAL FUSILIERS

Instructions regarding War Diaries and Intelligence Summaries are contained in F. S. Regs. Part II. and the Staff Manual respectively. Title pages will be prepared in manuscript.

Place	Date	Hour	Summary of Events and Information	Remarks and references to Appendices
LE QUESNOY	Jan 14		Nos. 2 and 4 companies salvaged the areas allotted to them. Nos. 1 and 3 companies were engaged on guards and fatigues.	
	Jan 15		Nos. 1 and 3 companies salvaged the areas allotted to them, Nos. 2 and 4 companies being engaged on guards and fatigues.	
	Jan 16		Nos. 2 and 4 companies salvaged the areas allotted to them. Nos. 1 and 3 companies were engaged on guards and fatigues. The Battalion was on duty for the Brigade.	
	Jan 17		Nos. 1 and 3 companies salvaged the areas allotted to them. The remainder of the Battalion were engaged on guards and fatigues. Captain H.C.W. Angled rejoined Battalion from sick leave.	
	Jan 18		No Salvaging was done on this day. The Battalion attended a lecture on "Demobilization and Reconstruction" in the morning.	
	Jan 19		No Salvaging. The Battalion paraded for Divine Service.	
	Jan 20		No Salvaging. The Battalion was engaged on Guards and fatigues. Lieut. B.W. Tanner M.C. and 54 O. Ranks proceeded to the Base for demobilization.	

Army Form C. 2118.

WAR DIARY
or
INTELLIGENCE SUMMARY, 3rd ROYAL FUSILIERS
(Erase heading not required.)

Instructions regarding War Diaries and Intelligence Summaries are contained in F. S. Regs., Part II. and the Staff Manual respectively. Title pages will be prepared in manuscript.

Place	Date	Hour	Summary of Events and Information	Remarks and references to Appendices
LE QUESNOY	Jan. 21		Nos. 1 and 3 Companies salvaged the areas allotted to them - the remainder of the Battalion being engaged in Guards and fatigues. 2/Lieutenant J.T. Morris rejoined Battalion from Area Commandant DOUAI. Major W.R. Lavender M.C. proceeded on leave to U.K. Sd	
	Jan. 22		Nos. 2 and 4 Companies salvaged the areas allotted to them, the remainder of the Battalion being engaged in Guards and fatigues. The Battalion was on duty for the Brigade. Sd	
	Jan. 23		There was no salvaging, the Battalion being engaged on Guards and fatigues. 2nd Lieut. F.R. Roberts rejoined Battalion from Area Commandant DOUAI. Sd	
	Jan. 24		Nos. 2 and 4 Companies salvaged the areas allotted to them; the remainder of the Battalion was on Guards and fatigues. Lieut. Colonel G. & F. Warren, Military Attache at TEHERAN gave a lecture to the Brigade in the afternoon on "The Caucasus and Russian fronts and the BAGDAD - BAKU Road". Sd	
	Jan. 25		Nos. 1 and 3 Companies salvaged the areas allotted to them. The remainder of the Battalion was engaged in Guards and fatigues. The Battalion found Brigade duties. Sd	
	Jan. 26		The Battalion paraded for Church parade in the morning. There was no salvaging duties. 2/Lieut. M.S. Francis left the Battalion for dispersal to the U.K. Sd	

Army Form C. 2118.

WAR DIARY
or
INTELLIGENCE SUMMARY.   3RD ROYAL FUSILIERS

(Erase heading not required.)

Instructions regarding War Diaries and Intelligence Summaries are contained in F. S. Regs., Part II. and the Staff Manual respectively. Title pages will be prepared in manuscript.

Place	Date	Hour	Summary of Events and Information	Remarks and references to Appendices
LE QUESNOY	Jan 26 (cont.)		2/Lieut. R.G. O'Neill rejoined Battalion from hospital. AW.	
	Jan 27		The Commanding Officer relinquished temporary command of the Brigade and resumed command of the Battalion. Nos. 1 and 3 companies salvaged the areas allotted to them, the remainder of the Battalion being engaged in Guards and Fatigues. AW.	
	Jan 28		The Commanding Officer proceeded to NAMUR. Nos. 2 and 4 companies salvaged the areas allotted to them, the remainder of the Battalion being engaged on Guards and Fatigues. The Battalion found Brigade duties. 2/Lieut. B.H. Roberts left the Battalion to take over duties of Area Commandant - VILLERS POL. AW.	
	Jan 29		Nos. 1 and 2 companies salvaged the areas allotted to them, the remainder of the Battalion was engaged in Guards and Fatigues. 2/Lieut. J.W. Mee rejoined the Battalion from Area Commandant VILLERS POL. AW.	
	Jan 30		The Commanding Officer returned from NAMUR. Nos. 3 and 4 companies salvaged the areas allotted to them, the remainder of the Battalion being engaged in Guards, Fatigues, and Brigade duties. AW.	

Army Form C. 2118.

WAR DIARY
or
INTELLIGENCE SUMMARY. 3RD ROYAL FUSILIERS.

(Erase heading not required.)

Instructions regarding War Diaries and Intelligence Summaries are contained in F. S. Regs., Part II. and the Staff Manual respectively. Title pages will be prepared in manuscript.

Place	Date	Hour	Summary of Events and Information	Remarks and references to Appendices
LE QUESNOY	Jan 31.		Nos. 1 and 2 companies salvaged the areas allotted to them – the remainder of the Battalion was engaged in Guards and fatigues. 2/Lieut. G.L.H. Intesani left the Battalion for an Educational Officers' course at OXFORD. Battalion Fighting Strength:- Officers 25 O. Ranks. 418 Admitted to hospitals during the month:- With Malaria – 2. Other causes – 14. AS. MoMahon Lt Col Cmdg 3/Royal Fusiliers	

(6392) Wt. W6192/P875 1,500,000 4/18 McA & W Ltd (E 2815) Forms W3091/4.   Army Form W.3091

50.C.
(8 sheets)

Cover for Documents.

Nature of Enclosures.

War Diary.

3RD ROYAL FUSILIERS.

February - 1919.

Appendices — Nil.

Notes, or Letters written.

Army Form C. 2118.

WAR DIARY
or
INTELLIGENCE SUMMARY.

(Erase heading not required.)

3RD ROYAL FUSILIERS.

Instructions regarding War Diaries and Intelligence Summaries are contained in F.S. Regs., Part II. and the Staff Manual respectively. Title pages will be prepared in manuscript.

Place	Date	Hour	Summary of Events and Information	Remarks and references to Appendices
LE QUESNOY	Feb 1.		Nos. 3 and 4 companies salvaged the areas allotted to them. The remainder of the Battalion engaged in Guards and fatigues. The Battalion was on duty for the Brigade.	
	Feb 2.		The Battalion paraded for Divine Service in the morning. There was no parading on this day.	
	Feb 3.		The companies were at the disposal of Company Commanders during the morning. There was no parading on this day.	
	Feb 4.		Nos. 1 and 2 companies salvaged the areas allotted to them, the remainder of the Battalion being engaged in Guards and fatigues. The Battalion was on Brigade duty. 2/Lieut. E.B. Brown left the Battalion for duty at XIII the Corps Demobilization Camp.	
	Feb 5.		Nos. 3 and 4 companies salvaged the areas allotted to them, the remainder of the Battalion was engaged in Guards and fatigues. 2/Lieut. H. Land rejoined the Battalion from a Chemistry course at DOULLENS. 2/Lieut. W.B. Turner admitted to hospital. 2/Lieut. H.W. Howell rejoined Battalion from leave in U.K. 2/Lieut. R. Murray to W.O. for dispersal.	

Army Form C. 2118.

WAR DIARY
or
INTELLIGENCE SUMMARY.   3RD ROYAL FUSILIERS.
(Erase heading not required.)

Place	Date	Hour	Summary of Events and Information	Remarks and references to Appendices
LE QUESNOY.	Feb. 6.		Nos. 1 and 2 companies salvaged the areas allotted to them; the remainder of the Battalion was engaged in parades and fatigues. 2/Lieut. R. Stanway left the Battalion for dispersal in U.K. The Concert Party gave a revised edition of the Revue "Hello - 1919" in the Regimental Theatre. Lieut. J. Ant rejoined Battalion from Dieppe.	
	Feb. 7.		Nos. 3 and 4 companies salvaged the areas allotted to them - the remainder of the Battalion was engaged in various fatigues and duties.	
	Feb. 8.		There was no salvaging on this day. The Battalion was on duty for the Brigade.	
	Feb. 9.		The Battalion paraded for Divine Service in the morning. There was no salvaging. Major W.R. Tresanton M.C. rejoined Battalion from leave in U.K.	
	Feb. 10.		Nos. 1 and 2 companies salvaged the areas allotted to them - the remainder of the Battalion being engaged in Brigade duties. Lieut. Colonel M.O. Clarke D.S.O. left Battalion for leave in U.K. 2/Lieut. J.H. Mee and 2/Lieut. A.W. Atwell were admitted to hospital.	

Army Form C. 2118.

WAR DIARY
or
INTELLIGENCE SUMMARY.

3RD ROYAL FUSILIERS.

(Erase heading not required.)

Instructions regarding War Diaries and Intelligence Summaries are contained in F. S. Regs. Part II. and the Staff Manual respectively. Title pages will be prepared in manuscript.

Place	Date	Hour	Summary of Events and Information	Remarks and references to Appendices
LE QUESNOY	Feb 10 (cont.)		The Royal Engineers' Band gave a concert in the Regimental Theatre during the afternoon.	
	Feb 11		There was no salvaging on this day. The Battalion was engaged on various duties and fatigues. 2/Lieut. E.W. Bone M.C. rejoined the Battalion from leave in United Kingdom. 2/Lieut. J.J. Morris left Battalion for leave in U.K.	
	Feb 12		There was no salvaging on this day. The Commanding Officer inspected the men of the Battalion earmarked for the Army of Occupation during the morning. The "LENA ASHWELL" Concert Party gave a performance in the Theatre during the evening	
	Feb 13		Nos 3 and 4 companies salvaged the areas allotted to them during the morning – the remainder of the Battalion being engaged for Brigade duties. 2/Lieut. E.W. Bone. M.C. admitted to hospital.	
	Feb 14		There was no salvaging on this day. The Battalion was engaged in duties and fatigues. 2/Lieut. J. Morrison rejoined the Battalion from hospital.	

Army Form C. 2118.

WAR DIARY

~~INTELLIGENCE SUMMARY~~

3RD ROYAL FUSILIERS

(Erase heading not required.)

Instructions regarding War Diaries and Intelligence Summaries are contained in F. S. Regs., Part II. and the Staff Manual respectively. Title pages will be prepared in manuscript.

Place	Date	Hour	Summary of Events and Information	Remarks and references to Appendices
LE QUESNOY	Feb 15.		There was no salvaging this day. During the morning the Divisional Commander inspected the draft for the army of Occupation. 2/Lieut. C.F. Heaton rejoined the Battalion from hospital.	
	Feb 16.		The Battalion Paraded for Divine Service in the morning. The Battalion was on duty for the Brigade. 2/Lieut. S.H. Roberts rejoined the Battalion from Area Commandant at VILLERS POL.	
	Feb 17.		The Battalion was engaged in various duties and fatigues. There was no salvaging.	
	Feb 18.		2/Lieut. R.G. le Maistre left the Battalion for leave in the U.K. The Battalion was engaged in ordinary daily routine.	
	Feb 19.		The Battalion was on duty for the Brigade.	
	Feb 20.		The Battalion was engaged in ordinary daily routine.	
	Feb 21.		The Battalion was engaged in ordinary daily routine.	
	Feb 22.		The Battalion was on duty for the Brigade. A "LENA ASHWELL Concert Party" gave a performance at the Regimental Theatre during the evening.	

Army Form C. 2118.

WAR DIARY
or
INTELLIGENCE SUMMARY.   3RD ROYAL FUSILIERS.
(Erase heading not required.)

Place	Date	Hour	Summary of Events and Information	Remarks and references to Appendices
LE QUESNOY	Feb 23		The Battalion paraded for Divine Service during the morning. Captain R.E. Ludvey and Lieut. J. Hart left the Battalion for the U.K. as Conducting Officers with a draft for demobilisation.	
	Feb 24.		The Battalion was engaged in ordinary daily routine.	
	Feb 25.		The Battalion was on duty for the Brigade. 2/Lieut. F.W. Bone. M.C. rejoined the Battalion from hospital.	
	Feb 26.		The Battalion was engaged in ordinary daily routine.	
	Feb 27		A draft of 10 Officers and 127 Other Ranks left the Battalion to join the 4th Battalion for duty with the army of occupation in Germany. The Officers were :- 2/Lieut. H.J. Stevens. M.C. 2/Lieut. F.W. Bone. M.C. 2/Lieut. J.H. Ford. 2/Lieut. R.J. O'Hair. 2/Lieut. J.A. Warren 2/Lieut. J. Morrison. 2/Lieut. G.E. Dumond 2/Lieut. C.L. Newton Lieut. J.J. Morris and 2/Lieut. R.J. Le Maistre were on leave and had orders to proceed to 4th Battalion direct. The remainder of the Battalion were engaged in ordinary daily routine.	

Army Form C. 2118.

WAR DIARY
or
INTELLIGENCE SUMMARY.   3RD ROYAL FUSILIERS.

(Erase heading not required.)

Place	Date	Hour	Summary of Events and Information	Remarks and references to Appendices
LE QUESNOY	Feb 28th		The Battalion was on duty for the Brigade for 24 hours commencing 28th inst. 2/Lieut. P.M.M. Rogers was admitted to hospital. Battalion fighting strength :- Officers – 16 O. Ranks – 196 Admitted to hospital during month :- With malaria – Nil Other causes – 14 [signature] Asst Adjutant 3rd Bn. Royal Fusiliers	

Vol 10

War Diary.
3rd Bn. Royal Fusiliers.
March 1919.

51C.
(7 sheets)

WAR DIARY or INTELLIGENCE SUMMARY

Army Form C. 2118.

3rd Bn. Royal Fusiliers

Place	Date	Hour	Summary of Events and Information	Remarks and references to Appendices
LE-QUESNOY	Mar 1st		The Battalion was engaged in ordinary daily routine. 2nd Lieutenant C.L. Farrott left the Battalion for duty as Embarking Officer to a draft for disposal in the United Kingdom. Summer Time commenced at 23.00 hours on this day.	
	Mar 2nd		The Battalion paraded for Divine Service in the morning.	
	Mar 3rd		The Battalion was on duty for the Brigade.	
	Mar 4th		The Battalion was engaged in ordinary daily routine. Lieutenant S.A. Turner left the Battalion for leave in the United Kingdom. Captain C.M.L. Gordon M.C. took over the duties of Acting Adjutant vice W.A. Lancaster M.C., Captain. 2/Lt Taylor, Lieutenant Lt/Major Ord and Lieutenant C.A. McCarron joined	
			Brussels on leave from Battalion.	
	Mar 5th		The Battalion was engaged in ordinary daily routine.	
	Mar 6th		The Battalion was engaged in ordinary daily routine. Major W.H. Grounds M.C., Captain C.B. Hughes, Lieutenant L.F. Moon, 2nd Lieutenant C.A. McCarron rejoined the Battalion from leave in Brussels.	

WAR DIARY
or
INTELLIGENCE SUMMARY.

Army Form C. 2118.

3rd Bn Royal Fusiliers

Place	Date	Hour	Summary of Events and Information	Remarks and references to Appendices
LE-QUESNOY	Mar 1st		The Battalion was engaged in ordinary daily routine. Captain Hon. A.D. Young left the Battalion for dispersal in United Kingdom. Lieut. A.L. Avery D.C.M., Lieut E.L.S. Page left the Battalion for duty as conducting officers with a draft for dispersal in the United Kingdom. Lieut S.J. McEwan, left the Battalion for duty with 19th F.A. W. Cay.	
	Mar 2nd		The Battalion was engaged in ordinary daily routine. Major W.G. Stocker M.C. Captain A. McF. Gordon M.C., Lieut. S. Lewis left the Battalion for leave in Brussels.	
	Mar 3rd		The Battalion paraded for divine service in the morning. Major W.G. Brewster M.C. Captain A. McF. Gordon M.C., Lieut. W. Stuart joined the Battalion from leave in Brussels.	
	Mar 4th		The Battalion was engaged in ordinary daily routine.	
	Mar 5th		The Battalion was engaged in ordinary daily routine. Lieut L.A. Roberts left the Battalion for duty as conducting officer to a draft of animals proceeding to Dieppe for demobilization.	
	Mar 6th		The Commanding Officer inspected the kits of the N.C.Os and men selected for the Cadre of the Battalion. Lieut W. Lewis, left the Battalion for duty as conducting officer with a draft of men and animals proceeding to Dieppe for demobilization.	

WAR DIARY or INTELLIGENCE SUMMARY.

Army Form C. 2118.

3rd Bn Royal Fusiliers.

(Erase heading not required.)

Place	Date	Hour	Summary of Events and Information	Remarks and references to Appendices
LE-QUESNOY	Mar 13th		The Battalion was engaged in ordinary daily routine. Lt-Colonel M.S. Clarke D.S.O. was granted an extension of leave from 13th March to 26th March.	
	Mar 14th		The Battalion was engaged in ordinary daily routine.	
	Mar 15th		Lt. Col. L.D.B. Gordon Hunt Cy. U.S.B. left Battalion for despatch in the United Kingdom.	
			The Battalion was engaged in ordinary daily routine.	
	Mar 16th		The Battalion paraded for Divine Service in the morning.	
	Mar 17th		The Battalion was engaged in ordinary daily routine. Lieut E.A. Roberts joined the Battalion from Animal Embarking duty.	
	Mar 18th		Lieut. D. Lewis joined the Battalion from Animal Embarking duty. The Battalion was engaged in ordinary daily routine. Lieut E.D. Gibson rejoined the Battalion from an Education course in U.K. Lieut L.A. Roberts left the Battalion on Cadre at L.H. Havaire.	
	Mar 19th		The Battalion was engaged in ordinary daily routine.	
	Mar 20th		The Battalion was engaged in ordinary daily routine. Captain R.C. Reding joined the Battalion from Brig't Embarking duty to the U.K.	
	Mar 21st		The Battalion was engaged in ordinary daily routine.	

WAR DIARY or INTELLIGENCE SUMMARY

Army Form C. 2118.

3rd Bn. Royal Fusiliers.

(Erase heading not required.)

Place	Date	Hour	Summary of Events and Information	Remarks and references to Appendices
LE-QUESNOY	Mar 1st		The Battalion was engaged in ordinary daily routine. Lieut. L.S.A. Arkwright left the Battalion for Leave in Paris.	
	Mar 23rd		The Battalion paraded for Divine Service in the morning.	
	Mar 24th		Lieut. A.A. Scott rejoined the Battalion from draft conducting duty in the U.K. Lieut. L.S.A. Arkwright rejoined the Battalion from leave in Paris. Captain L.G. Gadney left the Battalion for dispersal in the U.K.	
	Mar 25th		The Battalion was engaged in ordinary daily routine.	
	Mar 26th		The Battalion was engaged in ordinary daily routine. All officers present with the Battalion attended a presentation of captured German Guns to the State by the Queenois. They were presented by Brigadier General T.H. Shoubridge. The School of the British Government to the "Maire" of Le Quesnoy.	
	Mar 27th		The Battalion was engaged in ordinary daily routine. Lt. Colonel M. Clarke D.S.O. rejoined the Battalion from leave in the U.K. and took over command of the Battalion from Major W.A. Todwater, M.C.	
	Mar 28th		The Battalion was engaged in ordinary daily routine. Lieut. Hos Lage rejoined the Battalion from duty as draft conducting officer to U.K.	

WAR DIARY

Army Form C. 2118.

3 Bn. Royal Fusiliers

Place	Date	Hour	Summary of Events and Information	Remarks and references to Appendices
LE-QUESNOY	Mar 30th		The Battalion was engaged in ordinary daily routine	
	Mar 31st		The Battalion paraded for Divine Service in the morning. Lt-Colonel M.C. Clarke DSO. left the Battalion to take over command of the 14th Bn. Royal Fusiliers. Major W.G. Forrester M.C. took over command of the Battalion. Lieut A.J. Garratt left the Battalion for dispersal in the United Kingdom.	
			Battalion fighting strength Officers 9 OR Ranks 89.	
			Admitted to Hospital during month — With Malaria — Nil Other causes — 4.	

[signature] Lieut
Adjutant 3rd Bn. Royal Fusiliers

3rd Battalion Royal Fusiliers.

War Diary.   April, 1919.

52 C.
(5 sheets)

WAR DIARY

INTELLIGENCE SUMMARY. 3rd Bn ROYAL FUSILIERS.

Army Form C. 2118.

Place	Date	Hour	Summary of Events and Information	Remarks and references to Appendices
Le Quesnoy	1/4/19		The Battalion was engaged in ordinary daily routine	
	2/4/19		The Battalion was engaged in ordinary daily routine	
	3/4/19		The Battalion was engaged in ordinary daily routine. Lieut A.L.Gowers D.L.M. proceeded	
			Battalion from Duty. Conducting Duty in United Kingdom.	
	4/4/19		The Battalion was engaged in ordinary daily routine. Lieut. A.A. Turner proceeded from	
			leave in United Kingdom. Lieut. E.D.A. Artisani, proceeded to GAUDRY awaiting	
			orders for demobilisation	
	5/4/19		The Battalion was engaged in ordinary daily routine. Lieut. E.D.A. Artisani returned	
			Battalion from Arrival awaiting duty.	
	6/4/19		The Battalion paraded at 11 o'clock for Divine Service. Lieut. C.A.D. Stark	
			granted indulgence leave to United Kingdom.	
	7/4/19		The Battalion was engaged in ordinary daily routine. Lieut. A.A. Turner, proceeded	
			to United Kingdom for Dispersal	
	8/4/19		The Battalion was engaged in ordinary daily routine. Lieut A.L.Gowers, D.L.M.	
			proceeded to H.Q. Le Report to Regimental Dept.	
	9/4/19		The Battalion was engaged in ordinary daily routine.	

WAR DIARY or INTELLIGENCE SUMMARY

Army Form C. 2118.

3rd Bn. ROYAL FUSILIERS

Instructions regarding War Diaries and Intelligence Summaries are contained in F.S. Regs., Part II. and the Staff Manual respectively. Title pages will be prepared in manuscript.

(Erase heading not required.)

Place	Date	Hour	Summary of Events and Information	Remarks and references to Appendices
Le Quesnoy	10/4/19		The Battalion was engaged in ordinary daily routine.	
"	11/4/19		The Battalion was engaged in ordinary daily routine.	
"	12/4/19		The Battalion was engaged in ordinary daily routine.	
"	13/4/19		The Battalion paraded for Divine Service at 10 hours. Lieut. Col. Smith returned to Battalion from Hospital.	
"	14/4/19		The Battalion was engaged in ordinary daily routine. The Battalion is below strength.	
"	15/4/19		The Cadre was engaged in ordinary daily routine.	
"	16/4/19		The Cadre was engaged in ordinary daily routine.	
"	17/4/19		The Cadre was engaged in ordinary daily routine.	
"	18/4/19		The Cadre was engaged in ordinary daily routine. Voluntary Services in morning for all troops.	
"	19/4/19		The Cadre was engaged in ordinary daily routine. Lieut. Col. M.A. Best, Lieut. D. Lewis M.C. and Lieut. E.B. Roberts started 14 days leave to United Kingdom.	
"	20/4/19		The Cadre paraded for Divine Service at 11 o hours.	
"	21/4/19		The Cadre was engaged in ordinary daily routine.	

Army Form C. 2118.

WAR DIARY
or
INTELLIGENCE SUMMARY. 3rd Bn. Royal Fusiliers.
(Erase heading not required.)

Place	Date	Hour	Summary of Events and Information	Remarks and references to Appendices
Le Quesnoy	22/4/19		The Bn. was engaged in ordinary daily routine. Lieut. H.S. Howell proceeded U.K.	
	23/4/19		Initial Cadres for disposal	
			The Bn. was engaged in ordinary daily routine.	
	24/4/19		The Bn. paraded at 11.30 hours for first gaine of Lectures of F.S.R. the Bn.	
	25/4/19		was engaged in ordinary daily routine.	
	26/4/19		The Bn. was engaged in ordinary daily routine.	
	27/4/19		The Bn. was engaged in ordinary daily routine.	
	28/4/19		The Bn. paraded at 11.30 hours for Divine Service. Lieut. L.W. Brent joined	
			The Bn. was engaged in ordinary daily routine.	
			The Battalion from Courcelles in U.K.	
	29/4/19		The Bn. was engaged in ordinary daily routine.	
	30/4/19		The Bn. was engaged in ordinary daily routine.	
			Battalion fighting strength. Admitted to hospital during month.	
			Officers 6 Malaria Nil	
			O. Ranks 72. Other Causes	

Adjutant 3rd Bn. Royal Fusiliers

WAR DIARY.
3rd BATTALION ROYAL FUSILIERS.
MAY 1919.

Army Form C. 2118.

WAR DIARY
INTELLIGENCE SUMMARY. 3rd Bn. ROYAL FUSILIERS.
(Erase heading not required.)

Instructions regarding War Diaries and Intelligence Summaries are contained in F. S. Regs., Part II. and the Staff Manual respectively. Title pages will be prepared in manuscript.

Place	Date	Hour	Summary of Events and Information	Remarks and references to Appendices
Le Quesnoy	1-5-19		The Badn. was engaged in ordinary daily routine. AmJ.	
	2.5.19		The Badn. was engaged in ordinary daily routine. AmJ.	
	3.5.19		The Badn. was engaged in ordinary daily routine. AmJ.	
	4.5.19		The Badn. paraded at 10.45 hours for Divine Service. AmJ.	
	5.5.19		The Badn. was engaged in ordinary daily routine. AmJ.	
	6.5.19		The Badn. was engaged in ordinary daily routine. Major W.A. Trevendier AmJ. started 14 days leave to U.K. Lieut. L.P. Murch. granted 14 days leave to U.K. Lieut.-Col. M.S.A. Best. returned from leave in U.K. AmJ.	
	7.5.19		The Badn. was engaged in ordinary daily routine. AmJ.	
	8.5.19		The Badn. was engaged in ordinary daily routine. AmJ.	
	9.5.19		The Badn. was engaged in ordinary daily routine. AmJ.	
	10.5.19		The Badn. was engaged in ordinary daily routine. AmJ.	
	11.5.19		The Badn. paraded at 10.45 hours for Divine Service. AmJ.	
	12.5.19		The Badn. was engaged in ordinary daily routine. AmJ.	
	13.5.19		The Badn. was engaged in ordinary daily routine. Lieut. A.D. Page. proceeded to U.K. for dispersal. AmJ.	

Army Form C. 2118.

WAR DIARY

INTELLIGENCE SUMMARY. 3rd BN ROYAL FUSILIERS

(Erase heading not required.)

Instructions regarding War Diaries and Intelligence Summaries are contained in F. S. Regs., Part II. and the Staff Manual respectively. Title pages will be prepared in manuscript.

Place	Date	Hour	Summary of Events and Information	Remarks and references to Appendices
Le Quesnoy	14/5/19		The Bade was engaged in ordinary daily routine. Amn.	
	15.5.19		The Bade was engaged in ordinary daily routine. Amn.	
	16.5.19		The Bade was engaged in ordinary daily routine. Amn.	
	17.5.19		The Bade was engaged in ordinary daily routine. Amn.	
	18.5.19		The Bade paraded at 10.45 hours for Divine Service. Amn.	
	19.5.19		The Bade was engaged in ordinary daily routine. Amn.	
	20.5.19		The Bade was engaged in ordinary daily routine. Amn.	
	21.5.19		The Bade was engaged in ordinary daily routine. Amn.	
	22.5.19		The Bade was engaged in ordinary daily routine. Lieut L.P.Murra. rejoined from leave in United Kingdom. Amn.	
	23.5.19		The Bade was engaged in ordinary daily routine. Amn.	
	24.5.19		The Bade was engaged in ordinary daily routine. Amn.	
	25.5.19		The Bade paraded at 10.45 hours for Divine Service. Amn.	
	26.5.19		The Bade was engaged in ordinary daily routine. Amn.	
	27.5.19		The Bade was engaged in ordinary daily routine. Amn.	

Army Form C. 2118.

WAR DIARY

INTELLIGENCE SUMMARY. 3rd BN. ROYAL FUSILIERS

(Erase heading not required.)

Instructions regarding War Diaries and Intelligence Summaries are contained in F. S. Regs., Part II. and the Staff Manual respectively. Title pages will be prepared in manuscript.

Place	Date	Hour	Summary of Events and Information	Remarks and references to Appendices
Le Quesnoy	28.5.19		The Battn. was engaged in ordinary daily routine. Major W.A. Chandler M.C. returned from leave in U.K. Lieut. L.D.C. Anderson, posted to 3rd Battalion Royal Dublin Fusiliers. AmS.	
	29.5.19		The Battn. was engaged in ordinary daily routine. AmS.	
	30.5.19		The Battn. was engaged in ordinary daily routine. AmS.	
	31.5.19		The Battn. was engaged in ordinary daily routine. AmS.	
			Battalion fighting strength. Officers 7 Other Ranks 83.	Admitted to hospital during month With Other Causes: 2 With Malaria: Nil

C.W. Gordon Captain,
Adjutant 3rd Bn Royal Fusiliers

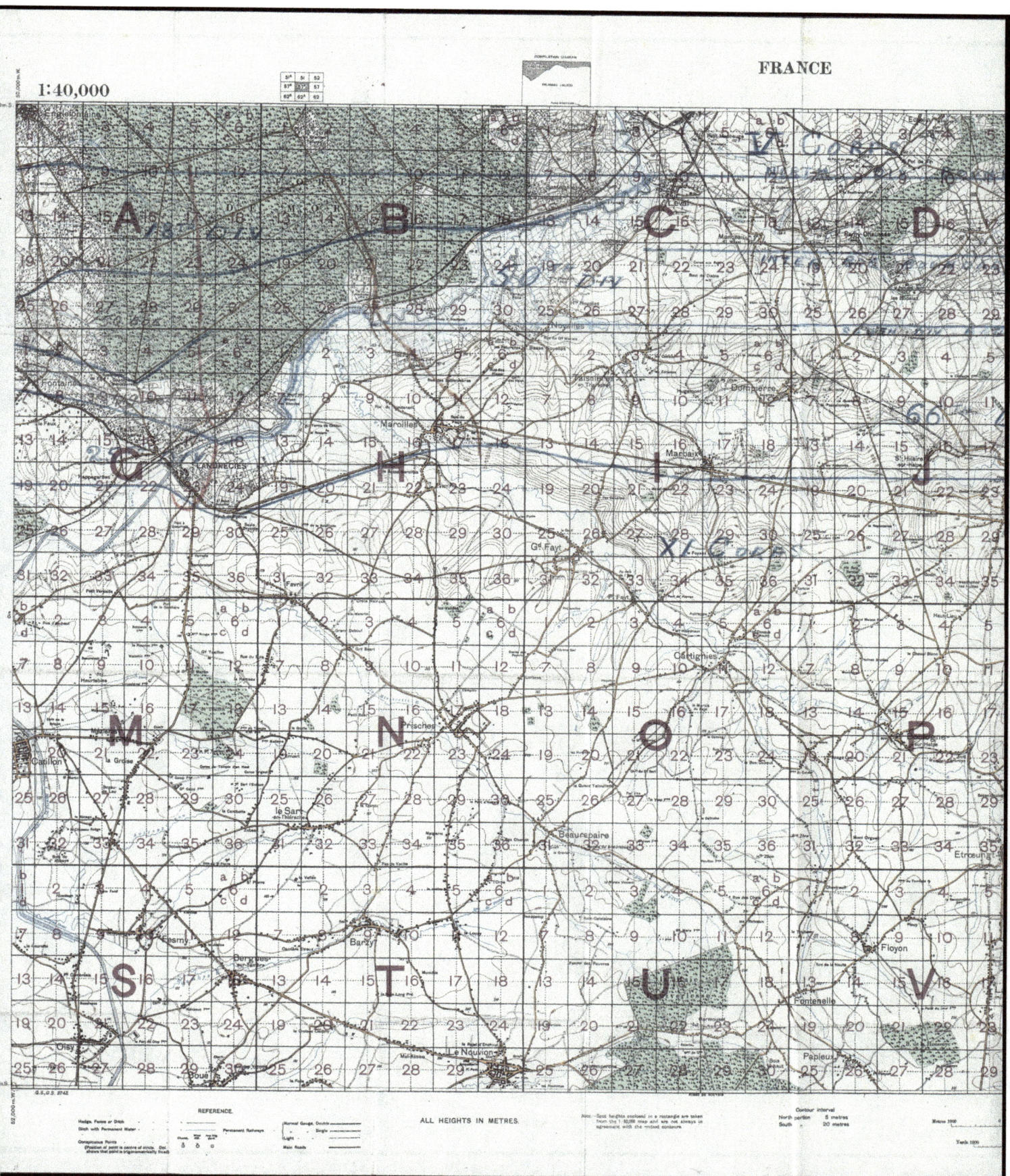

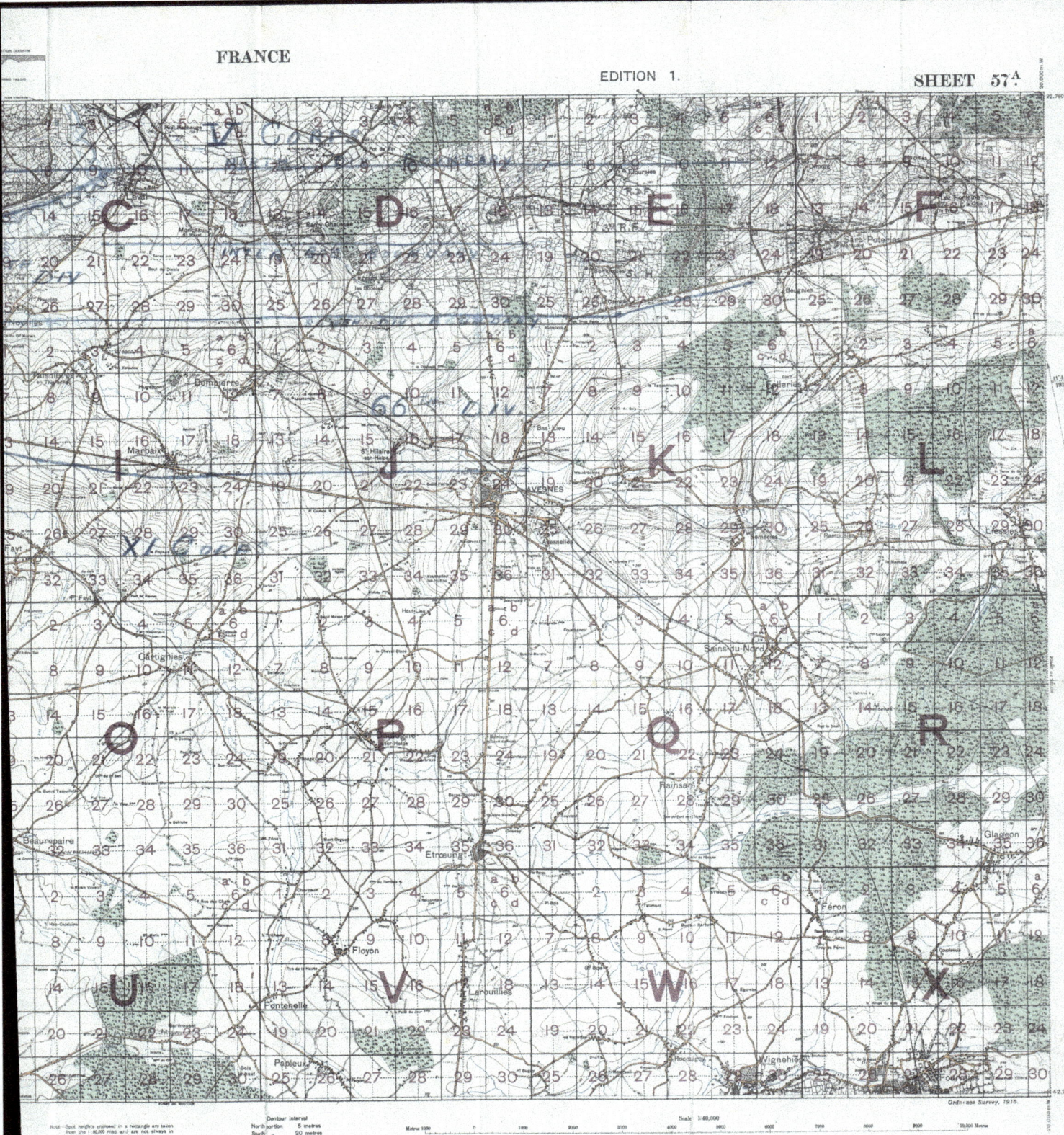

FRANCE.

SHEET 57ᴬ
EDITION 1.

INDEX TO ADJOINING SHEETS.

SCALE 1/40,000.

www.ingramcontent.com/pod-product-compliance
Lightning Source LLC
Chambersburg PA
CBHW081427160426
43193CB00013B/2213